Being One

Being One

finding our self in relationship

STEVEN HARRISON

A Crossroad Book
The Crossroad Publishing Company
New York

The Crossroad Publishing Company
370 Lexington Avenue
New York, NY 10017

Printed in the United States of America.

Library of Congress Cataloging-in-Publication Data

Harrison, Steven, 1954-
    Being one : finding our self in relationship / Steven Harrison.
        p.   cm.
    Includes bibliographical references.
    ISBN 0-8245-1681-8 (hardcover)
    1. Spiritual life. 2. Interpersonal relations—Religious aspects.
I. Title.
    BL626.33.H37   1999
    291.4'4—dc21   99-11109
                                                                 CIP

1   2   3   4   5   6   7   8   9   10   04   03   02   01   00   99

*This moment, this love comes to rest in me, many
beings in one being.
In one wheat grain a thousand sheaf stacks.
Inside the needle's eye a turning night of stars.*

—Rumi

contents

viii ❧ Contents

introduction

IN ORDER TO write this book, or perhaps more accurately, as a circumstance surrounding its creation, I have visited many forms of relationship over the past years.

During the period in which I wrote this book, I watched the birth of my first child and with that the emergence of a relationship of openness, innocence, and intimacy. This relationship demands everything and gives everything. It is love personified.

Sometime after the birth of my son, I went to the Himalayas for a solitary retreat. There, while continuing to write this book, my only companion was the powerful quality of aloneness and the vast expansion of consciousness that is its impersonal expression.

The context of the birth and the retreat and everything else that is my life is the confluence of individuals, some living together with me, some visiting, some who are met only briefly, but all of whom share in the inquiry. I have for many years met with people of all sorts to discuss the difficulties and questions of life and to come to the silence that occurs when the words have ceased.

By far, the questions most problematic to us all are the ones that relationship brings. So many people are confused and unhappy, and so much of it seems to be about relationship. In all these circumstances—the intimacy of a young child, the challenge of relationship in community, family, and marriage, and the intensity of solitude—I find myself writing about the same thing. The underlying issue remains the same in every circumstance. Will we be fully engaged in our lives, in our relationships? Is that our primary life mission, or are we focused only on survival, both psychological and material?

In the end I discover that it makes no difference whether I am bemoaning my fate as I change another diaper in the middle of the night or bemoaning my fate because I am halfway around the world from my son and missing his tiny/huge heart. The mind will always bemoan its fate. It will never be satisfied. Its nature is only conflicted. It is in conflict in relationship. It is in conflict alone. The cave of the recluse won't make us happy. The household won't make us happy. The mind cannot be happy.

Happiness grows only out of the profound silence in which the thoughts we call our self arise. In the moment our thoughts come still and just before the next thought arises—there, just there, is happiness. There, in the vast quiet, just there, is relationship.

Our lives can flow directly from this quiet, our circumstance can reflect it, our relationships can embody it.

This book is a collection of reflections and meditations on the nature of our world, as it is, and the possibilities of a world where relationship is realized as fact and separation is understood as deluded fiction. Through a book such as this perhaps communication, communing, can be triggered. That is this book's only intent; there is no other. This book may be a catalyst, but it is not the experiment. We are the experiment.

While the world our mind projects is pure illusion, life itself is not.

We still must live.

What we do with our lives, the very substance of our life energy, is where communication manifests, where communing takes form. This is the vast experiment of which we are all a vital part.

This book cannot take the reader to silence. It can only point out the nature of our minds. If silence comes, it comes on its own, it cannot be induced. There is nothing to be done. Silence is not causative.

This fact is entirely humbling for a mind used to creating results and effects from its efforts.

What is written here is about our self-delusion, and in the end that is the farthest that words can take us. This book has no answers in it and that is entirely deliberate. Instead, the book is a broad outline of a large question, the answer to which we will each need to live in our lives.✿

a story about love

THERE IS AN old Sufi story that goes something like this:

A young man was wandering from village to village, when he chanced upon the house of a young woman with whom he fell into mad love. He knocked on her door and from within the house her voice called out, "Who is it?"

"It is I," said the young man.

"Go away," said the woman, "There is not room enough in this house for two of us."

Devastated, the young man went away and did much penance, prayer, and meditation. Later, he returned and knocked on the door.

"Who is it?" came the voice from within the house.

"It is you."

The door opened.

4

living not alone

Everything that lives,
Lives not alone,
nor for itself.

—WILLIAM BLAKE

IT IS SELF-EVIDENT in a moment of stillness, in a quiet walk in the forest, in the beauty of a moonlit sky, that our lives are part of something immeasurable.

We know this. We know that we are both the teller of the tale and the expression of the story itself. We know that we are the meeting point of heaven and earth, the divine and the comic, the relative and the absolute. We can experience the divine in the depths of our humanness. We have the capacity to love.

We know this. But, we have forgotten it.

We have lost our way. We have lost our perspective. We have lost our understanding.

Like archaeologists of the soul, we begin to uncover the debris of our mind. Our need to exist in full relationship to our world is what drives us. The layer upon layer of ideas, conditioning, and fear is what we dig through.

In this search we have somehow forgotten that we have forgotten. The search has taken on a life of its own. The search has given us meaning that substitutes for what we have forgotten. But searching for love will not replace love. Nothing will replace love. If we forget everything else, let us remember that.

As we move through our life, as we uncover each stratum of mind, as we make our way through each reaction and discover each new aspect of understanding, can we remember that the expression of love is life itself?

The great discovery of the archaeology of the soul is that the search is over before it begins, because what we are looking for is what is looking. The wholeness of life is everywhere and is everything. We are already immersed in life and life in us.

In this we find that we do not need to discover love, that our being is one. But now we can discover because we love. And, because we love, we know that we live not alone.

Then why, we must ask, do we live as if we were alone?✵

alone:
the isolation of me

If you are afraid of loneliness, don't marry.

—ANTON CHEKHOV

AT SOME POINT we experience ourselves as distinct and separate beings. Despite the profound impact of this point of differentiation, we know nothing about it. This moment of individuation is lost in our personal history and in time.

Perhaps the point of separation is a primal awareness in the womb, or the moment of emergence into the outside world. Perhaps it is the first gasp for breath, for the vital air without which we will die.

Or, perhaps, it is the first hunger, the experience of the body-emptiness, the need for food-energy to fill us.

Or do we first experience our distinctiveness, our separation, as we experience discomfort and pain for the first time? We are cold, or wet, or hurt, and we don't yet have words or explanations for what is happening.

We may not remember what the first experience of separation was, but it is separation that most clearly defines us and most profoundly affects us.

We spend most of our early childhood exploring our separation, our distinctiveness relative to the world of external objects and internal drives. We emerge from an undifferentiated realm into a world we can affect. Reflex makes our toes curl. Instinct makes us call out when we are hungry. We begin to see a world that is related in some way to our wants. We begin to move our hands and feet, and soon we begin to move objects. We smile and our mother smiles back at us. We cry and someone comes running—to us. We are exploring relationship, but in that we are also discovering separation.

During our adolescence we actively develop our separation, cultivating our distinctiveness. If hair is generally kept long, we cut ours short. Or dye it green. Or make it stand on end. Anything, so long as we are different, separate. We may look for what includes us in groups, but even that search for acceptance is, in part, looking to stand out from some larger group. We trade a little individuation for a little group security.

As adults our separation gives us meaning and identity. We have struggled to define ourselves, and we have acquired the things that represent our personhood. We have a car that states who we are. We play music that expresses our taste. We dress according to our inner being. We have strong and original opinions on important matters. We have come to believe that we are true individuals.

We broker the separation of individuality into strategic alliances where we exchange bits of our autonomy for influence. We marry and our separation expands to include one other. Here we have given up something of our distinctiveness, but we have gotten, in return, some increased power, status, or security.

We work for a company where we give up some part of our distinctiveness in exchange for money. We join a religious organization where we adhere to a particular code of behavior in exchange for moral and, perhaps, cosmological security. We join a political party, support a candidate or cause, and form our opinions accordingly. We get in return power and influence. We believe that we are shaping our direction, our country's direction. We are sure of it. We feel safe. We are in control.

But, in fact, we can only move relative to our idea of separation, because we are so entrenched in it. We can only form strategic alliances, which strengthen the separate, distinct identity that we have cultivated throughout our lives.

Collectively, societally, we exist in a complex matrix of these alliances, a balancing act among competing forces. Like a monster turning on its creator, the matrix has subsumed the individuals. Born out of separation, this overlay of bartered individual needs has taken on a life of its own.

It has taken over the individuality, the clustered concepts of separation, and has created a prison. The prison is built upon the separation and dependent upon the separation, but is a collective force exerted upon the individual. This collective is unconscious. Because it is built upon separation, it embodies the loneliness, emptiness, and meaninglessness of that isolated state. Yet it is composite, controlling, and allows no true freedom. The societal matrix is the worst of both worlds.

In this complex ideation we are neither free individuals nor are we in relationship to the world around us. Instead, we have sold our freedom for security. We have sacrificed the intelligence of our own insight for the mass psychology. Most important, we have given up the dynamic possibilities and joy of relationship for our mechanical community of separation.

We are desperately alone. We have found our way from the undivided state of the womb to the individuated state of adulthood. We have become somebody, but we cannot find true contact anywhere in the world around us. Everything we touch turns into separation. We do not know anything else. We cannot conceive of anything else.

We marry out of loneliness and we end up lonely. We have children out of loneliness and we end up lonely. We have the family over for the holidays—the brothers and sisters, aunts and uncles, the parents—and we are lonely. We shop, we eat, we watch television, and we are lonely.

Our religion makes us lonely. Our job makes us lonely. Our therapist makes us lonely. Our music, our art, our writing make us lonely.

Do we ever admit this to ourselves? Do we admit to the desolation of our life? Or do we tell ourselves that it is all working, it all makes sense, it all has meaning? Do we keep moving, keep busy, keep full—full of activity, full of food, full of ourselves?

Are we full, or are we the fool?

It's not working. We aren't happy. We aren't in relationship. We are alone and lonely. We are empty, afraid, and dying the slow, agonizing death of avoidance.

What is the fear? What is the avoidance? We are alone, we are dying, we have no hope. We are looking away. We are sleeping, dreaming.

Does this dream have an ending? Are we left with the twilight world of living, but not living; living, but not loving?

Let us wake ourselves from the dream. In waking, where will we find ourselves? Who will we be?

If we are alone, we are distinct.

If we are in relationship, who are we?

If we are together, where is our boundary, our border?

Slowly, carefully, we rise from our slumber, blinking in the light of day. Our eyes focus and we begin to see.❦

the birth of the self

*It is well to remember that the entire
universe, with one trifling exception,
is composed of others.*

—JOHN ANDREW HOMES

WHERE DID THIS sense of separation come from? How did we get ourselves into this predicament? Did we think ourselves here?

As a child, a word or a concept is so novel that we play with it. We repeat the new word. We hear its sound, feel its quality, and observe its effect on others. A new word doesn't have substance because it has no history, no context, no purpose.

But once we are done playing with a word, when we have learned it, we store it for future use. When we use the word again, it is no longer fresh. We know all about the word and what it will do. Now it has become a technology for organizing and manipulating our world.

There is one more concept that we try out, feel, and eventually store away to use in a predictable way. This is the idea of self. We begin structuring our other ideas around a central organizing principle, a "me."

We have tried out this new idea on the world, and the world responded as if this self were real. This idea, this "me" became the backdrop of our reality.

What point is the point of this birth, the moment of distinction from the world around us? Can we find the moment of separation?

If we cannot find that point, if we cannot remember the moment where we moved from undivided to divided, from commingled to distinct, then how is it that we are so separate? How is it that we are so sure that we are separate?

The arising of thought gives the impression of separation. Thought, by its nature, divides. Its function is to create separation, distinction. The basis of our intellect is separating, categorizing. Our identification with the thought process gives us the impression that we are separate.

Yet if we pay attention to the field of consciousness in which thought arises, we can find no separation. The field of consciousness is apparently boundaryless. This vast, undivided awareness is available to us at all times. It is there at any moment we are still. It is as present in us as our thoughts. But we identify with thoughts, which are limited and separating by nature. Why is it that we do not identify with the field of consciousness, the milieu in which these thoughts arise?

Consciousness is only the background because we have neglected it in the busyness of our thought world, the conceptual framework in which we exist. The totality of life, the all and everything in which our thoughts occur and of which our thoughts are part, is not the background. This is so simply because there is no foreground, there is no separation, this is no thing that is not enfolded in the whole.

There is nothing outside of everything, and while we may create and identify with subsets of everything, even this attempt to divide is absorbed.

There is nothing outside of everything. All that we are left with is being. Being has no subject or object. It has no "thingness." Being subsumes everything. It is the universe as it is.

In being, there is only unity. It is the Self that the self forgot in early childhood. It is the love that we all seek in relationship to another. It is the mystic expression that religion seeks to convey.

In being, we discover our Self in relationship—not a relationship of time and space, but of two melded into one, self into Self, doing into being.❦

the body, birth, and death

There is nothing so unthinkable as thought, unless it is the absence of thought.

—SAMUEL BUTLER

EVEN MORE SO than our thoughts, our bodies give us the impression of separation. Our impulses, desires, and feelings are related to the body, its pleasures and pain, its survival. We seem to wake up to the same body. We seem to go to sleep with the same body. But do we? Is it the same body now as it was when we were children? Will it be the same body when we are aged and dying? Are our bodily drives and impulses a function of some discrete quality that we possess, something innately individual, or are they the collective expression of biology, genetics, and conditioning?

The ant observed from our perspective has a separate body but does not exist in separation. It is clear that the ant's body is integrally part of the ant colony. Further inspection shows the ant colony as an integral part of the ecological structure of the forest, the forest of the region, the region of the continent, the continent of the planet, and the planet of the universe. The ant's body is inextricably linked to the universe. It cannot be separated.

Our bodies, no less than the ant's, are part of the whole. Our bodies cannot be separated from the whole. When we breathe, the universe breathes. We are the whole.

If we do not have our thoughts or our body to give us our identity, then what separates us? We apparently exist as the meeting point of consciousness and the field of matter (in which the body exists). The field of energy, of consciousness, is infinite. The material field is infinite. We create ourselves through the identification with the finite, the nexus of energy and matter, which we call our selves. This basic identification seems to create the thought/body in which we exist until the dissolution in death.

To glimpse directly the nature of the self-creation, we must find death—the point of dissolution. By silent observation we can see that consciousness, when in contact with the body, gives us a sense of being.

We cannot directly know anything about death without going to the point where consciousness is no longer in contact with the body. Consciousness without an object is also consciousness without a "me." Without materiality, consciousness exists innately in its own sense of being and without separation. This is the expression of life without a center, without a thinker. It is death only

in the absence of the "me," not in the absence of life itself.

❧

There was a man who was burdened by a long life
of too many problems and too little money. One day, as
he was looking through all of his accumulated and over-
due bills, he threw everything off of his desk onto the
floor and shouted, "It would better if I were dead!"

The Angel of Death is always waiting for such a
call and arrived instantly.

"I am the Angel of Death," he said to the man.
"Why have you called me here?"

Frightened, the man replied, "Please help me put
all the bills back on my desk."

❧

Death is the thing we fear the most, the thing we
cannot comprehend and will not face. Death is the end
of our separation, our identity, our surety. Death appears
to us as the passageway to this vast field of consciousness, unobstructed by our form. But, it is the form with
which we identify.

We are fascinated by this possibility—the universe
without us. What would that be like? We investigate the
outer fringes of death: we get high on drugs and feel we
are losing our identity; we experience orgasmic sex and
lose ourselves for a moment; we meditate and feel we

have merged with the universe for twenty minutes; we take up dangerous sports and feel the rush of the nearness of death.

But in all these experiences, we know we will come back. We want to come back. The point *is* to come back, and not actually to die. We are not experiencing death, we are avoiding it.

Drugs wear off. Orgasms subside. Meditation comes to an end. We come back—to ourselves, our conditioning, our separation, our sorrow, our denial.

The whole syndrome—fear of death, flirting with death, avoidance of death—is illusion. We have never found our point of birth, our moment of separation. If we cannot find our birth, how will we die? What will die?

Is there a point of death, if there is no point of birth? If we cannot find a solid self in our minds or our bodies, then what is it that will dissolve in death? Is what we fear in death, the end of our separation, already a fact? What is not born cannot die. Death has already claimed that which is not actual.

Find the point of birth and at that moment death will be revealed. The alpha and omega are the same. That point of birth and death is this very moment, this very word, which falls away into absolute stillness.🌿

hope:
the projection
of together

*Hope is the only universal liar who
never loses his reputation for
veracity.*

—Robert Inggersoll

WE ARE ALONE, mechanically moving through our life of "quiet desperation." We rise to an alarm clock, we stimulate ourselves with caffeine and nicotine, we motivate ourselves with the latest book or video of promises. We get through our day, in order to get through the week, when we can get our paycheck, pay our bills, and go out for a night or two of drinking and looking for a mate.

What do we hope to find? We think that this mythic mate will remove our emptiness, fill our life, and make the loneliness go away.

Hope creates the expectation that in another we will find the missing pieces of our life. Hope assures us that we will provide the missing pieces for the other, as well. Our life will be perfect, we will be happy, and it will all be worth it.

Then our alarm goes off. It is Monday morning and time to go to work and begin another day in an endless series of days of our life. Hope forgot about this—our real life.

Hope has forgotten that we have not had an honest day in so long we have lost our sense of what it is like to not compromise.

Hope has forgotten that all our energy—physical and psychic—goes to the acquisition, maintenance, organization, and display of material things.

Hope has forgotten that we hide our physical imperfections under makeup, hairstyles, and clothing. We hide our psychological imperfections under therapy, denial, avoidance. We hide our spiritual imperfections under our surface religious practices and our glib intellect.

Hope has forgotten that we are deceiving ourselves, because we have forgotten our own deceptions.

How does a fraud meet someone who will bring happiness, who will bring fulfillment?

The fraud can trick the other into infatuation. This is easy. It is done with smoke and mirrors, compliments and deep looks, the deception of interest and attention. It is not hard to trick the other into loving, but the fraud can never love the one who has been tricked.

The fraud could, instead, reveal the true nature of the deceit to the other, but then, how could the other ever love the fraud?

We know we are deceiving ourselves. We know that our hope is also a deception. We are hopeless. The best we can expect is to meet another lost in this deception and fool each other so successfully that we can coexist in mutual denial.

It is Friday. Time to head out for a night on the town and, perhaps, to meet the other. We know this could be the night. We also know that this will never be the night. We dance. We forget.

The alarm clock goes off. It is Monday morning and time to go to work. We are alone. We go to work. We hope this week will be better. Hope has already forgotten everything as it anticipates the Friday ahead.

What happens if we see, in a moment, all the days of working in anticipation of the end of the week? What if, in a moment, we strip away the facade of affected personality? What happens if we face the missing parts of ourselves?

What if we take a new lover, one that will be with us always—our aloneness?

We can't do that. It is too painful, too frightening. We cannot bear the feeling of the emptiness, the aloneness. We need a warm body, something, anything, to fill up the space. We don't want to deal with this right now. Later we will be stronger, when we have a mate. Then we will face all of these feelings.

The alarm goes off. It is Monday morning and time to go to work. We hope this week will be better. We hope. We forget.❧

infatuation: the promise of contact

Love is the triumph of imagination over intelligence.

—H. L. MENCKEN

WHY IS IT that when we meet another we are suddenly without presence? We become bumbling fools where once stood a reasonably capable intellect. We become self-conscious, and the self, of which we have become conscious, is an embarrassing shell of a human being.

We are concerned about our impact on the other's mind. Will he like us? Will she be attracted?

We begin to see our flaws amplified and can only believe that this is what the other sees, too. If we can successfully hide those flaws and present the good parts, the other can only like us. But who is it that the other likes? Part of us—the part of us that anyone would like, if it were only true, if it were only whole.

Meanwhile, this other to whom we are attracted, and whom we are trying to attract, is presenting us with only the parts that we will like. Here is the sense of humor, but let's not look at the anger just now. Here is the creativity, but we won't mention the boredom. Here is the power and beauty, but not the insecurity and fear—not now.

If we are successful, we will seduce the other and the other will seduce us. So fooled, we will call it love and announce it to the world.

How long will this infatuation of fakery last? Will it survive the revelations to the other of all the things we have been hiding? Will it survive the revelation of all that the other has been hiding from us? Will we still be loved when we are seen to be what we are: afraid, self-centered, and manipulative? Will we still love when we see that the other is the same?

We know that the path of deceit can only lead to isolation. Perhaps this is why we are nervous when we meet the other. And we know from the beginning that we are on the path of deceit. We know that love requires honesty, and yet we are not honest. We know love requires deep contact with the other, but neither do we demand that contact nor do we give it.

We come to accept our deceit because love means the absolute end of narcissism, of the self-centered world, and as Samuel Johnson observed, our idea of an agreeable person is one who agrees with us.

✣

In Greek mythology Narcissus is unable to respond to the love of the wood nymphs, ignoring them in his self-centered life. One day he comes upon a clear, still pond in the middle of the forest and for the first time gazes at his own reflection.

He falls in love—with his own image.

He begs the reflected image to come to him, but, of course, it cannot. He reaches into the pond to touch his beloved, and his beloved withdraws. He remains at the side of the pond, gazing, in love, but unable to make contact.

Narcissus dies at that spot, and in his place grows the water-loving flower known as the narcissus.

Narcissus was destroyed by his total infatuation with his own image reflected in the water. Narcissus projected into that reflected image all his fantasies, the qualities that he found fascinating and alluring. His fascination paralyzed him. He was unable to move, to interact, to explore, to question. He could no longer be honest about himself or his beloved, which was, in fact, his projected image. He no longer cared. No one could convince him otherwise; no one could penetrate the circular argument of his self-love.

Viewing this love, we can see that it is not love at all but addictive self-involvement. But from within the state, we are convinced that it is true.

Narcissus is so secure in his delusion that he literally roots in it, forever hanging over the pond where the blossoming narcissus is reflected.

The narcissistic fallacy is not in the obsession with the self, but in the loss of the context in which the self is reflected. Narcissus could not see the pond in the forest, just as he could not see the rest of the world in which he existed and in which his reflection existed. Without this context there is no relationship, only the singularity of a self-centered fragment of the world.

We hope to find this perfectly reflected self in another. We hope to find a world that is made up of only the two of us. We hope to stare at our own reflection, gazing in raptured love, rooted in the spot, transfixed by ourselves. Most important, we hope that as we gaze, we will see this perfect reflection looking back with equal adoration.

We will then forget all the pain and discord, as will our perfect other. We will have each other. We will have ourselves. What we will *not* have is relationship.

Infatuation has forgotten that this other is ourself. But we have not forgotten. We know. This knowledge breaks the spell. We see ourselves in the other, but as our smile turns to a grimace, we see that the other is in pain, too.

The pond has begun to ripple in the sudden wind. We wake from our dream and notice the forest, the sounds, the light. We are again aware of our context. The adoration has come to an end. We are alone.

Now the search for a relationship becomes the search for sleep, for the dream, for infatuation. We know it is not true, but the addictive drive is overpowering.

We must sleep and dream that we are gazing once again at a fascinating creature, just like us, who is gazing back.

We look for that creature at work, in the restaurant, at our church, at the bar. While we look, this creature is looking for us in all the same places.

We are stalking and being stalked simultaneously.

We will eventually find this reflective infatuation, or it will find us. It makes no difference because it is the same.

But we already know that the infatuation can't stay, that the reflection will begin to ripple and we will be alone once again.

And, once again, we will begin the search.

❧

When we are in the throes of infatuation, it is most certain that we are chemically altered. Something has happened to us. Our bodies are on fire. We are alive. We see and feel and hear everything with intensity. We are intoxicated.

For some of us, what we are looking for is this state of infatuation. We are not looking for relationship. We are looking for the stupor of untested love. When this state wears off, as it will, we will look elsewhere for it. Or we will attempt to rekindle the fire with fantasy, romance, and risk-taking in the relationship.

We become desperate for that feeling of euphoria, with our brains awash with biochemicals signaling that we are about to mate. When these chemicals fade, when the feelings fade, we frantically search for the way back. We are shaking, sweaty, uncontrollably anxious. We blame the other, we blame ourselves, we cry, we plead. We need it. We need it now. We are addicted.

What is it to which we are addicted? Is it the hormones, the neurotransmitters, the biochemical, morphine-like substances sloshing about in our brains? There are so many simpler ways to get high and stay high. We could jog and get the runner's high. We could ingest chemical substances, drugs, alcohol. We could sublimate our drives into the acquisition of money and get high buying things (or even higher by not buying things and having even more money).

Why do we find ourselves so attracted to the infatuation with the other? Why are we so addicted to a state of fantasy-projection where no contact with the other can be made?

Perhaps we are not addicted to feelings that come with infatuation but are instead addicted to the separation. Perhaps this addiction to separation is so fundamental to our nature, so deeply rooted, that it uses the other as a backdrop to its self-love.

We are not, after all, infatuated with the other, we are in love with ourselves. The other is used as a screen for our projector. We are ecstatic because we have filled the universe with ourselves. There is nothing else. And there is nothing else like the feeling of that self-filled universe. This is what we are addicted to, and this is separation. We are admiring our reflection in all directions, and our reflection smiles back at us.

Then the euphoria crashes. The sensations begin to dull. The world has impinged on our self-love, and we find ourselves suddenly in contact and sober. We feel the pain, the sorrow, and division. In our intoxication we thought that was all gone. Now, we remember.

The other is suddenly demanding, critical, questioning, and fearful. The other no longer glows with that special luminosity but instead seems drab, flawed, and repulsive. We feel depressed, directionless, and desperate. We can run. We can look for the new other, the one that will make us feel the infatuation again. We need to feel ourselves again. We need to find the bubble of self-love, the world where only we and the other exist, the world where only we exist. We need a fix, and we need it now.

This cycle will repeat itself endlessly.

Or we can face our addiction to separation, our addiction to ourselves.

We will crash. The biochemicals will cease. We will become depressed. The world of bright colors will become dingy with shades of gray.

The other will become defective, depleted, dispirited. Then we will see that this other is ourselves—defective, depleted, dispirited. We will see that we have never met the other, only ourselves. We have never entered into relationship, into dialog, into contact with the other. We have been too full of ourselves. Now we are empty. We are prepared, at last, to enter into relationship. The doorway is well marked. The sign says: Pain.❧

the pain of relationship

Love never dies of starvation, but
often of indigestion.

—Ninon de Lenclos

Pain emerges as the central theme of relationships built on hope, denial, and the search for infatuation. When we have searched long enough, we will capture others and hold them in our grip as they hold us.

We will be bound together in relationship by habit, need, and fear. We will feed each other adoration until we are both exhausted and depleted. Our hope for something better will fade. We will be left with what we started with—loneliness and pain. But now we have a companion in our misery.

We have his brutish habits, his lack of responsibility, his dirty socks. We have her complaining, her hysteria, her constant cleaning.

We scream at each other. We scream at ourselves. We scream, but we can't seem to wake up. We know that it is painful without this relationship, and we know that it is painful with this relationship. We are paralyzed.

How did we get to this grand disappointment? What happened? We saw in the other such promise, such beauty. We had such a direct experience of love, of expansion, of openness when we met. This vast open space was so intoxicating we never considered its nature. We instantly, unconsciously identified this feeling with the person we had just encountered. But was this so?

Where has the feeling of expansion been until the encounter? Is it dormant? Is it nonexistent? What is it about the encounter that actualizes the feeling or creates it? Why do we never ask ourselves these questions in the throes of our ecstasy?

We have only looked for this expanded feeling in another. We have never looked within our life as it is. We have never asked ourselves whether this vast feeling of connectedness, of safety, of surety, is available now, here, without anything, without another. We discover in this question an entirely different perspective, one that releases us from the pressure of pursuit and gifts us with the possibility of rest.

If this expanded feeling, this sense of love, is not causative, if it does not occur because of something, then we are freed from the burden of acting, of doing, of searching. We do not need to find someone to give us love. We have love already. We are immersed in it. We cannot avoid it. The only way we can miss the fact of love is by searching for it, by looking for someone who can give it to us.

The Sufi mystic poet Rumi suggested that we are all like fish driven by thirst, missing the fact that we are already immersed in the thing we seek. We desperately flail about when all we need do is swim, the natural expression of our being.

We are conditioned to this notion of another who will give us love. We believe with all our being that we have found love when we find the other. We have not found love. We have found a hopelessly flawed projection. We have found an impossible image. We have found an other who cannot possibly give us what we already have, what we have always had, and what we will always have. We have found the obscuration of our vision, the forgetting of our love, the overwhelming sleepiness of conditioning.

We have not found love. We have found contraction. We have shrunk the expansiveness of the universe into a bubble world consisting of me and the other. We become the center of the bubble, and all we see is a reflection of that center on the inner surface of the bubble. The shimmering world is perfect, it is just as we had hoped, it is all and everything. Then the bubble bursts.❧

the addiction of separation

*In love, one always begins by
deceiving oneself, and one always
ends by deceiving others; that is what
the world calls romance.*

—OSCAR WILDE

IN EVERY FORM of relationship that we enter into—in our family, at our work, in our social network—we are lost in our assertion of separation. While we may have felt something apparently special in these associations in the beginning, we soon lose this quality as our distinction supersedes our connectedness.

Let us examine the formation of every relationship by looking at one kind of relationship.

We all know the feeling of falling in love. This is infatuation, drunken love, nondiscrimination. We know such love is blind, but it is fun. We know that it cannot last, but we don't want to deal with the future. This is the first stage of relationship.

The second stage is when we have institutionalized our infatuation. We now have a marriage or a committed relationship. We have grabbed the drunken love and decided to fight to keep it, by fighting with each other. We fight. We make up. There are tensions, disputes, miscommunications, but we make it work. We may internalize the conflict, consuming tension like a fine, white wine and smiling our happy-face smile that all is well. It is not.

The attraction to this phase is the tension. The tension is about us. It gives us the sense of solidity and "meness" that was missing in the world of infatuation. Tension reinforces our importance in the universe and gives us a feeling of receiving attention.

When the tension builds and releases, when we argue and make up, when we fight and make love, when we withhold and then give, we feel very alive. We generally get very attached to this stage of relationship and, unconsciously, do our best to maintain it.

We are told by endless popular psychology books that we can get beyond the stage of conflict to a more mature relationship. Or we can create contracts with each other. Or we can learn techniques to return to infatuated love. Or we can put the sizzle back in our monogamy.

Of course, what the pop psychology books say is not true. We know that when we buy the books. If any of the easy, feel-good aphorisms were true, we would all do it and be endlessly and abundantly happy.

The fact is that we do not want any of these relationship-resolving techniques to work because we like the tension. Without the tension we would enter the third stage of relationship. Here the tension is not resolved, it is exhausted. We become so much a part of each other that our individuation becomes blurred. This third stage is not infatuated, because it knows the other. It is not in conflict, because it has become the other. This stage is seen as unexciting by the mind that is conditioned to conflict. We are conditioned by culture, biology, and experience to crave the tensions of the second stage of relationship. We find the still, potential energy of the third stage too subtle, too quiet.

Quite the contrary, this third phase of relationship is entirely dynamic. The energy of the relationship is no longer being expended on the creation and dissolution of separation. There is no one to fight with. The other has become an extension of ourselves. We are so resistant to this dynamic boredom that we immediately begin to fill the space in our relationships with division and conflict. Neurosis enters and fills the space. We feel alive once more. We feel our boundaries, our definitions, our individuality. We are safe.

In the infatuation stage we have no control. In the boredom stage we have no one to control. Only in the second stage of relationship, the conflict of separation, can we actually control the nature of our relationship. This is where our addiction resides, the addiction of separation.

Exhaustion is the only way out of the endless cycle of tension and release that is the addiction of separation. No addiction comes to full rest in the face of temptation, because the underlying structure of addiction is the divided world that temptation represents.

This addiction of separation limits every kind of relationship, every attempt to connect with the world around us.

Addiction can be transferred. We can trade coffee for cigarettes. Addiction can be sublimated. We can give up our sexual addiction and expend it instead on gaining power and money. Addiction can be withheld. Through religious zeal we can try to constrain our temptation. Addiction can be indulged. We can simply give in and enjoy the ride before we crash. But addiction cannot be resolved without a complete understanding of the world of duality. This divided world, the world of should and shouldn't, good and bad, addict and addiction, subject and object, is the problem.

Our addiction is to ourselves, to the concept of a "me" in relationship to a world of objects. Although we will not allow ourselves to question thoroughly and examine this structure of the me-centered world, we dedicate all of our energy to its maintenance.

We wake up craving separation. We splash water in our face and confirm our distinctiveness when we look in the mirror. We dress ourselves as an expression of our individualism. We go to work to assert our power. We court each other as an expression of our dominance or our seductiveness. We live in our separate dwellings, reveling in our freedom to choose whatever television program we want to watch.

This is the addiction of separation.

We have tried to go cold turkey, to break the habit, to get free of the compulsion.

We join a religion where we can agree with everyone about what God is, how to worship, what is right and wrong. We are relieved, we are free of our addiction, we are no longer separate. Then we walk by the other church or temple where we see the others believing something different. We are suddenly glad we went to our church, that we believe what we believe, that we worship the "right" god. Does this separation from those others who have chosen the "wrong" faith give us some small measure of security? The addiction is back, the addiction of separation.

We try to break the addiction. We find a lover. We let go of ourselves and experience the euphoria of relationship. We are finally free. We have found someone who is perfect in every way—except that little nervous habit he has of chewing on his pen. And, she's a little neurotic about money. Well, actually, very neurotic. In fact, the money issue is a major problem. And the cat— we are allergic to cats. And, he is depressed a lot. In fact, this relationship is not working that well; it may be time to think about a separation. Separation will solve all of this, just a little separation. Maybe a lot of separation. The addiction is back.

We gossip about our friends, we take our political positions, we complain about our work, our boss, our life, as if these expressions of self bring us relationship. We control our children in the name of parenting. We obsess about money as if worry creates security. We look the other way when we come across the destitute, the ill, the aged, the confused, as if looking away will bring us peace of mind. In each and every consideration we have of the world around us, we establish our distinction from it. We construct a place where we stand outside of the rest of life. From this imagined place we crave the very life from which we believe we are separated.✣

the end of wanting

Things will get better despite our
efforts to improve them.

—WILL ROGERS

THE ADDICT LOOKS at the object and says, "I want" and "I shouldn't." The tension of this divided world can only be resolved temporarily by indulging. But the addict again is faced with "I want" and "I shouldn't." Again and again the addict indulges.

Let us put the addict through rehabilitation. Now, the addict hears "I shouldn't" so loudly that "I want" is obscured. The addict is free from indulgence, but the price is the eternal negation of "I want," the suppression of the drive to experience. The addict is free of the destructive habit but unexpressed, unmanifest, and unfulfilled. Now the addiction is to "I shouldn't," and the addict must indulge in that as frequently as he once indulged his desires.

What if we take away the conflict, take away the "I shouldn't"? All that is left is the "I want." The "I want" is driven to acquire, to possess, to experience. The "I want" is me-centered, unconcerned with the world around, because there is no longer an "I shouldn't." The "I want" takes and takes. It feeds endlessly on its indulgence without ever being fulfilled. It consumes until bloated and, overloaded, it collapses of its own excesses.

Now, take the "I" out of the "I want." Take the center out of the perspective, the identity out of the impulse. Wanting without the "I" attached cannot find direction. It is without the intelligence to know what to devour. There is no "I shouldn't" to give it clues, because there is no "I." Wanting finds no joy in indulgence because its nature is to want, not to have. Its nature is to want, not to experience. Wanting has no past and no future. It cannot remember what it is looking for or why. It is not emptiness looking for fulfillment. It is not depression looking for happiness. It is not loneliness looking for relationship. It is wanting. Just wanting. Endlessly wanting.

There is nothing to do with or for wanting. It exists inherently in its own nature.

We have removed "I shouldn't" from the "I want—I shouldn't" addict and discovered indulgence and destruction. But we have continued by removing the "I." In that, we have come to a space where the wanting exists but has no action, no expression, no power, and it causes no harm.

We discover that the addiction is not to our desire. It is to our *self*.

Desire is not the problem. *We* are the problem.

Desire without identification, without "me," has no impetus. Addiction, without the addict, has no expression and so needs no suppression.

If the center, the "me," steps out of the arena of addiction, there is no fight. "Should" and "shouldn't" remain, but there is nothing that gives them energy.

This is the exhaustion of addiction and the exhaustion of "me."

transcendental relationship

*True love is like a ghost: everybody
talks about it, but few have seen it.*

—FRANÇOIS DE LA ROCHEFOUCAULD

THE IDEA OF stages of relationship is just that, an idea.
It is a way of talking about relationship, but it is not relationship itself. Language is not what it describes; it is symbolic or representational. It may convey accurately, but often it distorts, interprets, and confuses.

We are so in love with our words and ideas that we forget the direct experience from which language arises. We build concept upon concept. In the end we have abstracted our contact with life, a contact that is fresh and vital, into the rote regurgitation of thought-bound ideology.

When we use language like "the three stages of relationship," let us use that language, but then forget that we used it. Don't enshrine the language. Cremate it and scatter it in the wind. Or better yet, leave it for the vultures to pick over.

43

If the use of our created terminology or the classification of phenomena through conceptualization allows us a glimpse of the underlying structures of our life, that is fine. Otherwise, throw all the language out. Its usefulness is over.

We can try to figure out which stage we *are* in, which stage we *should* be in, which stage we *will* be in (if we just figure out which stage we should be in). But we are only in one stage—the stage of confusion.

One of the curses of human existence is the tendency to misconstrue language for actuality. Relationship has nothing to do with language, name, or concept. We cannot analyze relationship. We cannot control relationship. We are already in relationship, but our view is so obscured that we do not recognize that fact.

If we are particularly alert, sensitive, and open, we may discover this fact. We are already in relationship.

If we have not discovered this, if we do not fundamentally experience this in our moment-to-moment existence, then we have fallen victim to the great curse. We are stuck in language, concept, thought. We are entombed in our own brains.

We are *thinking* our lives, not *living* them. We are thinking love and relationship, not living them.

Now we think about the problems all this thought is creating.

We pick up a self-help book, a book of spiritual advice, a religious book. We pick up this very book, thinking it might help with our thought-bound world. We read about being one, and we think that is quite interesting.

We think we will read more, until we are reading this sentence. We are not sure where all of this is going, but we think we will read more and find out.

It is not going anywhere.

Thought has nowhere to go but its own isolated, endless, fragmented repetition.

Blow it up. Discard it. Take this book and rip out every page up to this sentence and throw them all away. Now throw away this page and sit still for just a minute without the obsession of thought.

❧

Now, read on with fresh eyes and the space of openness. In that freshness, with no past, no memory, no thought, we have entered into relationship. This is not the relating of a person to a person, of an ego-center to the object of its desire, of fear to the world it must try to control.

This relationship is transcendental. It is the recognition and the expression of the energy of consciousness and space in which we and the other coexist in such profound contact that there is nothing that definitively divides us.

The mother whose just-born child suckles her breast cannot say where her life and the child's are divided. The child's cry is the very energy of the mother's response to quiet him. The child's openness and intimacy are the reflection of the mother's own heart.

The lover who truly loves, the guru who truly shows the way, the teacher who truly mentors, the parent who truly guides, and then, each lets go—this is the reflection of relationship.

We search for this relationship of profound openness, without guile or armor, vulnerable, trusting and, at the same time, intimate, intertwined, boundaryless. This transcendental relationship constantly slips from us as we experience it and then try to institutionalize it. Relationship is the natural state of our being, when our minds are absolutely quiet. When thought is still, it is apparent that all of the world is in relationship. Then thought, the ego-center, enters immediately to catalog, analyze, and capture the beauty of the vision.

We seek the rare butterfly. Upon glimpsing its beauty we stalk it, catch it, drive a pin through its head to mount it, and put it on our wall with its Latin name. What we had was spontaneous beauty existing as freedom, not owned, not controlled. What we now have is a dead specimen.

Why do we trade the moment of timeless beauty for the endless stultification of a dead symbol, an artifact, a word, a concept?

We can use language here to approach that which is beyond language. We can use language here to amuse ourselves. We can use language as the poet does, as the bird sings its song. But, let us not forget that these words, any words, bring us nowhere in actuality, only somewhere in the mind, in thought.

To enter into this relatedness we need do nothing, we need know nothing, we need learn nothing. We are there already, now, here. For the active mind this is difficult to conceptualize.

To allow our minds to conceptualize this, we say we need help. We need books, teachers, courses—books on the philosophy of something that will help us understand nothingness. We need teachers of something, courses in the miracles of something, that will help us conceptualize this nothing. Slowly we start to get it. We think harder. The concept begins to gather its wits. At last, we understand nothing. We are so relieved finally to have a concept to hold onto. Even if it is nothing, at least it is something.

Soon, with study, with practice and, perhaps, with the grace of God or the guru, we get it. The concept is complete. We can explain it to our friends and family, we can teach others, we can gather power, prestige, and security. With our newly found concept of transcendental relatedness, who knows, we might even impress someone enough to get a relationship going.

We have an "ism" or an "osophy." Thank God, we are safe—unless there is no god in our concept, then we thank the stars, karma, or gaia. But where are we? Are we indeed where we conceptualized we should be, or are we back in the bubble, are we staring in the pond admiring the reflection of our own thoughts?

Let us find out where we are. Today, let us remove all concepts from our viewpoint and place them on a shelf (where they can easily be retrieved).

Now, let us begin our day.

What shall we wear? What shall we say? Are we happy today? Are we sad? Are we fulfilled? How is our life going?

Without our concepts, our patterns of belief, we are lost. There is no reference point. Without the concepts cluttering our view, we have no viewpoint, no vantage point, no place from which to "be." We cannot even become disoriented or afraid, because we cannot find these concepts.

❧

Supreme Court Justice Oliver Wendell Holmes was on a train when he discovered he had left his ticket at home. The conductor was more than accommodating, saying, "I'm sure the railroad can trust you. Just mail in the ticket later."

"Dear sir," replied Holmes, "that is not the problem. The problem is not where my ticket is. The problem is, *where am I going*?"

❧

Indeed, where are we going? We have nothing, which is what we have always had. There is no vantage point, but there is space. This space is not a concept (although we can try hard to make it one). It is empty of concept, empty of us.

This space transcends us, because it transcends our concepts. This space connects us, because in this space all actuality exists related not in a conceptual framework but in existential reality.

We have lost ourselves in nothing, and we have found our existence stripped bare of everything but its interrelatedness. We are not *in* relationship, we *are* relationship. In this moment we glimpse that this is the simple nature of what is. It has always been so, with or without our view or understanding.

This radically changes relationship to another, because we find no entry point to relationship and no exit from it. We cannot look for relationship; there is nothing to see that is not already in relationship. We cannot get anything from relationship; we already hold everything. We have no place to go and nothing to do.

Then thought arises. What about me? Where did I leave those concepts? Aha, here they are. What an experience I've just had. That was so profound, perhaps now I'll be happy. After all, that was a very special experience.

This is thought.

Wake up. Love does not sleep, we do.❦

fear:
the breakdown
of separation

All the passions seek whatever
nourishes them: fear loves the idea of
danger.

—JOSEPH JOUBERT

SEPARATION CANNOT BREAK down simply because it does not actually exist outside of the nature of our viewpoint. Our viewpoint sustains the idea of separation through repetitive, obsessive reinforcement of the notion.

Through the world of emotion—hurt, anger, fear, happiness, and all the rest—thought relates to a world outside itself. It creates separation by the force of its own projection. It creates a psychological center that has thoughts and feelings about a world which is interacting with the center. Where is the world? Where is the center?

The center, the self, is delineated by fear. We know where we are, because we know what we fear. The fear defines what is ours, what is safe, what is unthreatened. It tells us who are our mates, our children, our family, our friends. Outside of this sphere of fear is the unknown. The unknown is what we must never see, or touch, or try. We will certainly be destroyed by it. Our brains are inflamed by the fear of what will happen if we enter the unknown. It is, after all, terribly, awfully, indescribably, fearfully, unknown.

Why does the unknown create such angst? The unknown is not really what it seems. It is not even unknown. What is truly unknown can generate no quality in our minds, because it does not yet have any quality. What is truly unknown cannot generate fear. What, then, is creating all of the fear by which we guide our lives?

Into the null set, the unknown, our minds project what fear tells us is there. This dark closet of our mind contains the memory of our failures, our hurts, our anxieties. This is the known, the repeating litany of the past by which we try to navigate the future. We cannot bear the thought of the unknown, not because it is empty, but because it is filled with our known. It is filled with us, and we are in pain.

We are trapped in that pain and by the projection of the pain into the unknown. If we change we will be in pain, or so we project. If we don't change, we will be in pain, but at least it is the pain we know, the pain we identify as our self. The battered wife who is unwilling to leave her husband is the clearest example of accepting the familiar pain, of finding security in the pain that we know. But we all accept the conflict that we know over the uncertainty of a direction beyond the known.

If we understand this construction, we can begin to see the nature of freedom. The unknown is the portal to freedom. The life of freedom is fresh and vital simply because it is *not* the past, the repetition, the known.

We do not need to choose between the pain of our current lives and the fear of the unknown. The pain of our current life *is* the fear of the unknown, and as such we are liberated simply by embracing that unknown in each and every moment of our life.

We do not need to fear contact with the world around us, we need to fear the world of psychological and physical isolation in which we now live and from which we derive our fragile sense of security.

What will happen if we live—if we quit the dead-end job, if we leave the loveless marriage, if we say no to the spoiled child or demanding parent? Will we die a horrible death, will we starve, will we go homeless, if we live a life of radical creativity and love?

Fear says that we will die. Fear says that we will starve. Fear says that we will be old and sick and that no one will take care of us. Fear has looked hard at the life of freedom, feeling, and passion and declared it unfit for human habitation.

The fact is that fear is what is unfit for human habitation. Fear needs to be condemned and torn down. Yet

we allow fear to operate our lives, and we live, with res-
ignation, in the soul squalor of fear.

To face our fear, we must face our death. To pre-
pare ourselves to die, to glimpse our death, to live in the
imminence of our death is the end of fear. But our biggest fear, the fear we run from the hardest, the fear we
spend our lives avoiding, is the fear of death. We know
we will die. The body will fall away. The possessions we
have gathered and protected so diligently will turn to
dust. The money we have worked for and hoarded so
frugally will be dissipated. The parents, the spouse, the
children, the friends will all die, too. The churning of life
will include death for everything we have, everything
we have become, everything we know.

Death comes not just at the end of our life; it comes
every moment. Look closely at the thought-body, at the
mind as it creates reality through the arising of thought.
Thought arises, but then it passes away. The universe is
created and destroyed. Observe this carefully.

Fear is created and destroyed as it arises and passes
away in the mind as thought. It has no substance outside of this arising and the habitual attraction that we
feel toward it. Without our attraction to it, our identification with it, our belief in it, fear has no energy and
simply withers into the emptiness of a quiet mind. Fear
dies. The fear of death dies. We die.

We are liberated by this realization, by this death.
What dies is not life; what dies are our impediments to
the expression of that life. Life expresses itself in us and
through us in this death. Because our fear dies, the

unknown is born as the very expression of life in the freshness of each moment.

With the death of fear and the death of the fear of death comes the end of separation. We can no longer be afraid of the unknown encounter, the unknown relationship, the unknown love. We can no longer live in fear and the boundaries that fear draws around us. We can no longer find the delineations that fear made between us and them, between our family and the rest of humanity, between our job and the rest of our life, between our country and the rest of the world, between our backyard and the rest of the world environment. As we examine the inner world of thoughts and feelings, we can no longer find the distinction between the conscious and the unconscious, between original thoughts and conditioned thoughts, between what is distinctly us and what is the collective mind.

Now, to live in separation, to design our lives in separation, no longer works. We have entered the realm of radical creativity where our art becomes the life we live, the forms we express, the very communication of the undivided energy we have discovered through the living experiment of our self.

Fear says that it cannot be done, it cannot be lived. Fear says that separation is the fact of survival. But we have nothing to say to fear anymore. Fear is dead. We are living.❧

love as the great confrontation

Heaven's net is vast;
Though its meshes are wide,
nothing escapes.

—TAO TE CHING

THERE IS NOTHING in relationship more powerful than the expression of love.

We may think power in a relationship comes from the critical eye for the other's flaws. We spend a great deal of our energy in our relationships finding the hypocrisies and foibles of our partner. This, we believe, gives us the ability to intimidate, to control, to gain power over the other.

But criticism can be absorbed by the other. The other may be distorted or scarred by this but still remain intact as a separate entity. The construction of the self is such that it can absorb the positive and the negative equally well, so long as the self is the focus of the attention.

55

This is why the endless varieties of destructive relationships exist and continue. Each party to the relationship can feed off the energy of the other. The relationship is not about happiness, fulfillment, or integration but about the "me" maintaining its existence. Like a parasite, the "me" is concerned about the host only in that the host must be kept alive to feed the parasite.

This is why love is so powerful. The expression of love, all-encompassing, non-separate love, cannot be absorbed. It shatters the other as it shatters us. It is the most powerful and the most avoided energy. In love there is no "me." The parasite dies; the host lives.

How is it that we manage our lives so as to avoid love? After all, we say love is all we really want. We say we would give anything to have love and to express love. But we do not have or express love; we evade it. We live our lives in avoidance of the very thing we say we want.

We avoid love because love ends our autonomy. It expands our boundaries to such a vast degree that our boundaries cease to exist. We are no longer ourselves. We are not distinct and separate.

In love we are in relationship and, in relationship, everything is in contact with everything else, everything is part of everything else. We are not separate in love, and in truth, what we love is our separation. We cannot give it up, even though it is destroying us.

Let us go "cold turkey" with our addiction of separation. Now, despite our withdrawal symptoms, the cold sweats, the overwhelming compulsion to hide from each other, we commit to radical honesty and full disclosure of who we are. We demand that from the other, and we refuse to accommodate less.

What happens? We have created a firestorm of veracity, and everything that is false begins to burn in it. The false in our world begins to fall away. Our world begins to fall away. *We* begin to fall away.

Fear arises as our world shifts. It tempts us with the safety and security of a little compromise, a concession here, some negotiation there. Our family pressures us, our spouse threatens us, our friends stop calling. Fear tells us that if we continue with this radical honesty business we will be alone for the rest of our lives. We begin to crumble. We will have just one little compromise. We can handle it. It won't really affect us.

Let us wait a moment, before we have that one little compromise. What if fear is right and we are alone? What would that really be like? Why does that drive us to concede our integrity, over and over throughout our life?

Before we reach for the accommodation of dishonesty, let us explore our aloneness. If it is truly unbearable, then the politics of compromise will still be waiting for us. Our family will forgive us, our spouse will accept us again, our friends will start calling. We can go home to our hidden place where fear will warn us if honesty ever tries to approach again.

We say we want love. We know we are terrified of its implications, its demands of honesty and integrity.

We tell ourselves that we risk a terrible loneliness if we expose ourselves with honesty.

Now, let us experience that loneliness.

If we are truly interested in cutting through the stuff of the mind to the stuff of the heart, let us face the loneliness. Where is it?

It must be found in being physically alone. So, let us take our two weeks' vacation and be physically alone. Go to a cabin. Go to a mountaintop. Go to a river. Go to an island.

Don't take a class in loneliness. Don't find someone to guide the way through. Don't take a book. Don't take this book. Go without anything and be there. Watch the mind bring up its demons and angels, its fears and hopes, its good and bad. We don't have to do anything with the stuff of the mind, because we are alone. We don't have to express it, and we don't have to suppress it. When loneliness comes, we don't have to do anything with it. Soon, we are terribly lonely. We still don't have to do anything with it. Sometimes our mind gets quiet. We don't have to do anything with that quiet. Sometimes we feel the depths of the universe and the overwhelming love expressing from it. We don't have to do anything with that love.

The mind stuff goes on in our place of loneliness. In our retreat, our place away from our life, we discover that we will not die of loneliness. In our retreat, or after we have left our retreat, we also discover that we do not need a place away from our life to experience the loneliness of our life. We find that the simple act of observation, without denial or avoidance, brings us into contact with that loneliness, wherever we are. We cannot cover it with activity, and we cannot discover it by inactivity. The loneliness has become our companion, our lover. We merge, and suddenly, loneliness is transformed. Through the direct contact and exploration of our loneliness, we have extracted our fear. We are no longer lonely. Now we are alone.

Aloneness is fearless. It is the ground on which we may enter into relationship with the world around us. Aloneness has the integrity of needing nothing.

Aloneness has sat still and watched the river flow by.

Aloneness has looked through its closets of possessions, its Rolodex of relationships, its bank accounts, retirement plans, and health-insurance policies. Aloneness doesn't need any of it. Aloneness has experienced the neurosis of a dependent marriage, dependent children, dependent parents.

Aloneness has seen the pathos of disease and dying, the silence of death.

Aloneness has seen the endless chatter of the mind and the vast stillness of the field of consciousness that frames and permeates each thought.

Aloneness needs nothing, and so has everything. It doesn't crave to be filled by another, and so is in relationship.

Aloneness is the transformer through which consciousness flows to become love.

This love is the message of the universe. It is the truth of the universe. Yet, it cannot be touched by those who crave, who desire, who want. Only when we have found the absolute contentment of aloneness can we give expression to love. This is our purification.

It is good that we are purified, because love confronts everything about us that is false or divided. It strips us down to the essential beingness that underlies our conditioned state. This love is a jealous mistress who rages if we have eyes for anyone else, even ourselves. This love is the creator, sustainer, and destroyer. Love is everything and, as such, cannot be contained by anything.

We asked for it. We got it. We are in love. There is no way out. ❧

love is a dangerous word

> *When my love swears that she is made*
> *of truth, I do believe her, though I*
> *know she lies.*
>
> —WILLIAM SHAKESPEARE

LOVE DOES NOT exist. Love is a word. Love is a concept. Love has attached to it every memory, idea, image we have associated with it since we first heard the word.

Love to us means romance, it means attention, it means altruism, it means biological family, it means some spiritual goal we have set forth for ourselves.

Even in this book the word *love* is used frequently and seems to allude to a state we can achieve through some understanding or proper course of action.

Love is a dangerous word. We delude ourselves with it. We so easily confuse ourselves with this word.

Remember, it is a word.

Love is a word.

Love is a concept.

Love does not actually exist.

It is simple. Love is a description of what is beyond words.

Love is a word used because we don't have any words left.

Love is the absence of the speaker, the thinker, the reality that attends language itself. It is the state that is a non-state, a quality that has no attributes and no perceiver of attributes. Because it is undivided, it cannot be touched by thought. Thought only exists in division. It cannot be remembered as it is, but only as it is conceptualized.

So, when we come to love, we must throw out this last thing, this last idea. Whatever we call love, we must throw it out. Throw out the good feeling around the word; throw out the bad feeling for not having the word.

Throw out love. It is not actual. There is nothing that is love. Nothing is love. Love is nothing.

This is the frontier beyond which nothing can help us—no teacher, no theory, no philosophy, no book. This is the space beyond language and beyond us.

It cannot be described. It can only be lived. Life exists in wholeness arising spontaneously, without words, without thought, without love. ❧

authentic aloneness

I have three chairs in my house: one
for solitude, two for friendship, three
for company.

—HENRY DAVID THOREAU

IMAGINE FOR A moment that we have everything we need. We are not lacking anything materially or psychologically. Imagine, further, that because we have everything we need, we don't want anything.

Now, imagine how that state of "no need" would change our lives and, in particular, how we act in relationships.

In this imaginary world there can be no blame, because there is no lack. There is no craving, because there is no lack. There is no insecurity, because there is no lack.

Relationship in this imaginary world is dramatically different from the relationships we now know. In our new world relationships are not transactional, there is no deal happening, there is no contract. Since we don't need anything, we don't have to extract anything from the other. We don't need attention, or adulation, or feed-back, or sex, or money.

In our new world we have nothing to lose by be-ing completely honest in our expression and unarmored in our reception. We don't have to behave in a different manner when we are with another than when we are alone. We are relieved of the anxiety of finding approval, of being liked, of being accepted, because we are per-fectly content being alone, being unapproved and unac-cepted.

We discover, in this imaginary world, that there is a tremendous access to all the energy we have been ex-pending in the pursuit of correct behavior. This energy is now available to us for creation, for health, for rela-tionship.

As our need to behave in particular ways falls away, a strange thing happens. We can no longer find ourselves. We have come to a still point, which we have called aloneness. From this we have discovered that we have all that we need in life and cannot extract anything from the world around us anyway. We have found that the patterns of behavior no longer apply, because those pat-terns were attempts at appeasement and solicitation, qualities we no longer need.

But if we are not grasping and cajoling, what is left of us that is recognizable?

Here we discover that we know nothing about ourselves outside of the conditioned patterns. We don't know what our capacities are, or what our potential is.

We don't know anything about ourselves other than that we are still, we are complete, and we are in relationship without need. We are no longer functioning in the context of life, but rather we are the expression of that context. The beauty of it is beyond description. It is beyond imagination.

What a wonderful world we have imagined, one that is beyond imagination. It is beyond imagination, because we have nothing in our experience that can tell us what that world is like. We know what this world is like, the world of deals, compromises, and survival. We cannot know what this world we have imagined is like.

And that is the beauty of this imaginary world. We cannot imagine it. We cannot project the past into it. We cannot bring the known of our scarred and sordid past into it.

We can only enter this new world, this world of authentic aloneness, with nothing. We can bring no history, no expectations, and no maps to guide us. We cannot use our ideas and theories to help us.

We can access this new world only now. We can encounter this world only by leaving the past. We find this world not by talking about it, reading about it, or discussing it, but by entering it.

We enter with no exit.

Alone, without psychological need, our contrivances of personality fall away. Only then can something authentic emerge. Only then can the silence speak.

Imagine that.❦

when one meets another

Lovers don't finally meet somewhere.
They're in each other all along.

—RUMI

IN A STORY from Jewish folklore, the sly old marriage broker is trying to match up the stubborn young man with a good wife.

"The one I have for you is a true beauty," says the broker to the young man.

"No thanks," says the man.

"All right, all right, then I have another one for you. She's no beauty, but she has plenty of money and a lot of property."

"Not interested," says the young man. "I have plenty of my own money."

"Ah, so it is connections you want. I have the perfect girl for you. She comes from a great and powerful family."

"Look," said the young man, "I am not interested in beauty, money, or connections. When I marry, it will be for love!"

"Well, as a matter of fact," said the marriage broker, "I happen to have one of those, too!"

✣

When one of us meets another in intimacy or marriage, a contract is signed. The deal might include tradeoffs, compromises, payments, and bonuses. One will look the other way at this. The other will look the other way at that. The contract is amended as time goes by and, unless there is a great deal of care, eventually becomes a voluminous mass of obligations and dishonesties.

When our relationship develops like this, the burden of these deals and subdeals becomes more and more ponderous, and more and more difficult to adhere to. Deals are broken, subdeals are forgotten. The once enamored couple now spend their time arguing over who has broken what clause in the addendum to the subcontract appending the master deal. They look for allies, confessors, counselors. They tell their tales of woe. But they won't give up their rights under the contract.

The contract is unspoken and unconscious. The contract calls for immaturity and dishonesty. The contract needs to be discarded.

It doesn't have to be this way.

When one of us meets another, there doesn't need to be a deal. Try honesty. Try maturity. Try being an adult. Throw out the contract, if there is one, and start over. If there isn't a contract, don't negotiate one.

Try a relationship that is based on freedom, that is not held together by anything at all. The relationship must be vital or it falls apart. It must be honest or it withers. It can't be based on the woman promising to be a girl or the man promising to be a boy—that requires a contract. It can't be based on the demands of one on the other and the counter demands of the other.

When one of us meets another in love, in intimacy, in marriage, let the relationship live in that meeting, in the freshness of the contact.

What is the risk in this? If we aren't bound by the contract of our relationship, what will happen? We risk the other person not responding in a predictable way, we risk the other contradicting our stance, we risk the effects on ourselves of direct, unconditioned communication from the other. We risk, in the end, losing all of the control, predictability, and protection we have built into the relationship, and every relationship into which we have ever entered.

We risk leaving the protected world of our own mind. This mental world was projected into the other, and the other agreed to abide by the rules. We never had to be concerned about leaving the safety of the known. Now we are going to put it all in jeopardy.

We withdraw the projection and void the agreement to abide by it. Our mental world exists now in relationship to the other and to the world around it. The tariffs are removed. This is the world of psychological free trade and mental open markets. Market forces come to bear, and what is artificial quickly falls away. What is real remains.

Our projected self is artificial. Nothing protects it. The other's projected self is artificial. Nothing protects it. This is the very thing we have shielded ourselves from all these years. We are in contact. We have no position. We have no control. We cannot contain what is happening. This is the risk we took when we removed the contract.

We got what we wanted, and we got what we did not want. We got relationship, but we got relationship. We are on the cutting edge, the brink, the edge of the abyss each and every moment. There are no guarantees to give and none to get. We are fully responsible for the entirety of our life.

Now we can look at the other with clear eyes. We can speak with an uncensored tongue. We can hear without reaction, or if there is reaction, we can hear that. We may discover that we are now in an intimate relationship. We may discover that we are in a contrivance of a relationship that is suddenly past tense. But we will discover precisely where we are. We will discover the fact, the actuality, of our relationship. This is the risk we took. It is terrifying. We have grown up. We are a man or a woman, and we require, we can do with no less than, another man or woman, if we are to be in intimate relationship. We may be of help to the adult boys and girls in our life, but intimacy is out of the question. Psychological children cannot give informed consent to such openness.

Counselors will tell us that psychological children can have relationships. These advisors tell us that these adult children of "psychoholics" just need to clarify their contracts with each other to make their relationships work. Nothing can make these relationships work until the adult children grow up and relate as adults. This is not a process. This is a moment. It is this moment, or it is never. The counselors of these aged children, the ones who sell them on time and on process, reinforce the child they claim to be liberating. There is no money to be made on timelessness, on immediacy. If we are convinced that these processes work, then let us hug our teddy bears and attend the seminars. After some time, after some process, and it doesn't make any difference how long a time or what the process, we still come to the same point. We are already at that point. We have always been at that point. The point is the abyss. The point is adulthood. The point is relationship.

Now we can find out what happens when we meet another.❧

sex and separation

The thing that takes up the least amount of time and causes the most amount of trouble is sex.

—JOHN BARRYMORE

 SEXUAL TENSION IS part of all of our relationships.

In some relationships the recognition of the sexual content is taboo, so we deny it. If the sexual taboo is expressed, we punish those who give it expression. Even if the taboo is discussed, we suppress it.

In some relationships the sexual content is accepted, but the expression is denied. In others the sexual content is recognized, and the expression of the sexual energy is accepted.

This is a curious thing. Why is this, of all body appetites, so carefully regulated and so severely punished?

Before we address this question, let us go to the planet Htrae as intergalactic anthropologists. On this planet we observe some fascinating phenomena.

71

Food is hoarded and controlled, even though it is abundant. The priests and politicians educate the population to the evils of experiencing hunger and the punishments for eating. Food is never talked about except in sarcastic food jokes or by snide reference. Food is never discussed around children.

Images of gourmet meals and fancy desserts are intermingled with most entertainment and advertising. The most popular entertainers openly eat for pleasure alone and sing about food and its carnal draw.

The politicians of Htrae, on the other hand, are never seen eating and certainly not for pleasure. They create strong laws regarding food and severely punish those who are caught eating too much, or choosing from the wrong food groups, or selling explicit pictures of food.

The religious leaders promise eternal damnation for eating, unless it is done in the manner condoned by the church's Holy Cookbook and after a proper ceremony. In this fascinating religious ceremony a person, who is of age, may promise, before family and friends, to eat only the church-prescribed foods, in the correct amounts of all five food groups, and only for the purpose of health. This vow is of obedience to the food laws of the church in sickness and health until death parts the individual from this world.

Our team of anthropologists observes other interesting food behaviors.

Some people eat only from one food group and are denied their political and church rights because of it. Most heteronutrients secretly believe that food-trans-mitted disease is God's punishment for being homo-nutrient.

There are bi-nutrients who eat just about anything. They believe all Htraeans are actually bi-nutrients and simply in denial.

The fundamentalist religious believers think heteronutrientism should be strictly enforced. There are also progressives who think everyone should be free to eat as he or she wishes, but the progressives don't know what to do about the ones who want to feed children, sell raunchy food pictures, and other deviations.

The world of Htrae is full of confusion about food and eating. It is rampant with botulism; secret, illegal restaurants; and malnutrition. The priests and politicians are busy.

As we leave Htrae, we cannot help feeling sad about a place so utterly perplexed about such simple matters.

We return to Earth, breathe a sigh of relief, and have a good meal. The waitress is attractive. We hope she notices us, but we don't say anything because it may be too forward. We have thoughts, but we really shouldn't have those thoughts, because we are married, after all. We suppress the urges we feel, but we keep watching the waitress out of the corner of our eye.

The latest music star is playing on the video moni-tor by the bar, selling something—sexy, half clothed, taunting. We go over to the bar for a drink, a closer look, and a fantasy.

We are definitely back on planet Earth.

❧

If sexual energy is a part of all of our relationships, why then is it so profoundly regulated, internally and externally?

Historically and biologically, sexual activity meant reproduction. Survival became dependent upon the stability of the family group, but a family group was not necessarily monogamous or a couple.

Our nearest kin, the monkeys and apes, seem to organize in stable, multi-member groups that slowly change as members age and come or go. Survival here is at a group or tribal level. Sexual behavior is utilized for reproduction, as a substitute for aggression, and as a release of general tension and boredom.

Perhaps for the human being, as the social situation became larger and more complicated, the survival strategies changed. A tribal unit could no longer be easily defined by the physical space that surrounded it. Religion and law began to express the sexual taboos that would prevent incestuous mutations; ensure reproductive, heterosexual activities; force fathers to identify and stay with their offspring; and ensure that land rights passed in an orderly process to the next generation.

Sexual energy was identified early on by the Christian church as a force to be harnessed and controlled. Doctrines regulating sexual behavior have become so embedded in our culture that we no longer question them. Through religion, the state began to exert control over sexual behavior.

Sexual freedom became the domain of the depraved and the powerful, those who ignored the law and those who were above it.

Sexuality was forced into the shadows. Those who stepped from the shadow were crushed. Those who learned to navigate in the shadows found power. Soon, sexual energy was converted to and expressed as power.

The destruction that we observe in many sexual expressions (and sexual predators of all kinds) is a function of power, control, and violence, not of sexuality. The historic social constraints on sexual behavior attempt to regulate this violence and, at the same time, inadvertently create it.

The constraints on sexual expression are changing now, in large part because sexual activity no longer necessarily equals reproduction. Further, it may be important, from a survival standpoint, that most sexual activity does not result in reproduction. If we segment sexual activity from reproduction, what are we left with? What laws and mores apply in a scientific age where we control pregnancy and birth? What if we, like our next of kin, the apes, constrain violence and not sex?

We can sort out the question only by moving through our own ideas, conditioning, and forms. We may begin to discover that our sexual energy is so deeply unconscious that we know almost nothing of it but our behavioral manifestations.

For these behaviors we have created categories. For these categories we have built complex descriptions, proscriptions, and advice. But these layers of thoughts about sexual energy have little to do with the energy itself. We are investigating the result of the energy rather than the energy. We will only understand a little about electricity by observing a shining light bulb.

We cannot understand anything about sexual energy without first discarding all of the misinformation, misunderstanding, and the rest of the dregs of the experts. We must first discard our own sexual identities, our own sexual conditioning, our own sexual presumptions. None of what we know is helpful.

Is there really such a thing as a homosexual, a bisexual, or a heterosexual? Who thought of these ideas anyway? These categories have nothing to do with sexual energy and everything to do with our conditioning.

We have learned behavior, and we have learned how to elicit behavior from each other. We watch the movies, we read the magazines, we listen in the locker room and the classroom.

We may associate our sexual energy with an attraction to a person, place, or thing. We may associate our sexual energy with an attraction to a category. We may associate sexual energy with power, control, or violence.

The human psyche loves the security of an identity, and so we love that we can so clearly claim our affiliation with some sexual group. We even love the affiliation with a group that exists merely to react to some other sexual group. In the name of God, morality, or psychiatry we pronounce our judgments on each other and the wide variety of expressions of sexual energy.

It is all conditioning, secondhand, and profoundly misguided confusion. We don't have anything to say about sex, other than the pap from psychological treatises, pop versions of the Kama Sutra, ninth-grade sex education classes, and religious dogma of various sorts.

Throw it all out!

If we want to discover the nature of sexual energy, first burn all the books that the Fundamentalists don't want us to read. Then burn all the books that the Fundamentalists do want us to read. Now we are free from the information, the categories, the ideas about sex.

We can begin to explore. Where does sexual energy occur for us? Is it in the genitals? Is it in the head? The heart? Let us find where in our bodies we experience this energy.

What do we associate with this energy? What images, ideas, feelings do we find when we experience sexual energy? If we are aware, we discover a dimension of this energy that is unlike anything we have categorized as sex.

We may discover that sexual energy is conditioned energy, conditioned by the images and ideas we have learned to associate with certain qualities or forms of our consciousness. As the energy of our consciousness comes into contact with particular body areas or mind formations, it is conditioned, shaped into a thought-bound form. What was undivided energy becomes divided.

The implantation of thought into consciousness divides consciousness. This fragmented world is inherently unstable and tense. It tends to recombination, which is the implantation of consciousness into thought and the return to the original wholeness.

This inherent tension is experienced in the sexual-physical area as a biological imperative to copulate and reproduce, to combine and create consciousness. In the sexual-psychological area this fragmentation is experienced as the feeling of isolation and the drive for relationship, the loneliness and projected fulfillment. In the sexual-social area this fragmentation/tension is experienced as the plethora of sexual identities, groupings, and dogmas that tend to divide from each other and, at the same time, are driven to conquer or absorb each other.

All of these apparent divisions are limited by the conditioning that creates them. Consciousness dispels division, not in dissolving them, but in the inherent awareness that transcends the divided state.

After all, it is discovered that sexual energy does not exist outside of the division of the conditioned mind.

Sex is energy that is polarized.

Sexual guilt is the blockage of this energy, as experienced from a center, a "me."

Without the experience of the center, there cannot be guilt or pleasure. Sexual energy without the center is not polarized. It is undifferentiated energy.

This undifferentiated energy is available to us all the time, with or without sex.

We look to sexual energy as a means to experience this undifferentiated energy. Through a sexual partner we experience the reflection of our polarization and the undifferentiated energy that results. Then we are polarized again.

We look for more sex, or more partners, and we are still polarized in the end.

Sexual energy is an endless cycle of attraction, combination, and polarization.

There is nothing wrong with this. It is not bad, evil, or sinful. We have been taught by religion that it is bad. We have been taught guilt. We have been taught by culture and media that it is pleasurable, powerful, forbidden, dangerous.

The fact is that it is simply an endless cycle. It is conditioned. It is not free.

The undifferentiated energy is always present. It is free and unconditioned. ❦

sex and tantra

> *What is peculiar to modern societies,*
> *in fact, is not that they consigned sex*
> *to a shadow existence, but that they*
> *dedicated themselves to speaking of it*
> *ad infinitum, while exploiting it as*
> the *secret.*
>
> —MICHEL FOUCAULT

WE HAVE BEEN trained from the dawning of our sexual awakening to relate to the sexual experience from an aspect. We are male or female. We are heterosexual or homosexual. We are dominating or submissive. We are driven by sex or revolted by it.

We may take on any of these aspects and perform within their constraints, but we are never really satisfied. We believe there must be more. The books and advisors tell us there is more.

The psychologists explain to us why we are the way we are and how to become better. Men are advised to find their wild man, their feminine man, their caveman. Women are told that they are to satisfy their man, romance

their man, find their man in themselves, or simply realize that they are from Venus. We are told how to find the
secrets to endless orgasms and erotic ecstasy. We are fascinated by all of this. We buy the books and tapes. We
become voyeurs reading about fantasy couples in per-
petual orgasmic rapture. But we are not living the fantasies we read about.

The New Age spiritual advisors tell us about Tantra.
This is it! There are rituals, arcane visualizations, meditations, and exotic gods and goddesses. We retain the
semen, absorb the orgasm, activate the thousand-petalled
lotus. Now we are getting somewhere! At the next party
we attend, we find ourselves working the subject of
Tantra into the conversation. What a great pick-up line,
what a way to show our stuff. This is the real thing. We've
read the books. It works. At least that's what the books
say. We actually haven't gotten very far with the reten-
tion thing, and that thousand-petalled lotus, well . . .
what are they talking about?

Why does this deep confusion continue? What are
we actually looking for? Why all the advice?

Here is some real advice. Let us be honest with
ourselves instead of constantly seeking advice. We are
not interested in sex. We're interested in orgasm. We're
interested in power. We're interested in control. We're
interested in infantile regression. We're interested in fantasy.

Sex is the means to another end. We are objects,
and the other is an object, and both are used to get to

that end. We are not interested in sexual energy because we have no idea what it is. We have never experienced it because it remains unconscious. We *are* interested in the results of that energy, the images we associate with that energy, the power we feel from that energy.

We have entered into arrangements with an other whom we have objectified, manipulated, and negotiated into a predictable pattern that we call relationship. It is safe, controllable. We take on an aspect of the relationship, and the other takes on an aspect. What is sex in this arrangement? It is a ritual predicated on our negotiations, a novel we have already read, a movie we have already seen too many times.

Psychology won't help us. Tantra won't help us. But total honesty will, because honesty will shatter our relationship. Honesty will shred the contract. Honesty will wake us up and strip away the concretized liturgy that our life has become.

Start from the beginning. We meet and there is sexual attraction. Can we stay with that energy, can we explore it, without falling into our patterned expression?

We are not an aspect of this energy. We don't need to take a role or submit to a role. We don't need to be terrified of this energy, nor are we compelled to express it. We don't need to overpower or seduce the other.

What happens when we simply stay conscious? We stay awake and present. We experience the sexual energy, ourselves, and the other without separation.

This is sex and orgasm and love—and we haven't even moved yet.

When we enter into sexual relations in an undivided state, we are involved in sexual energy unlike anything we have read about or experienced.

We don't need a role now. We don't need a fantasy. We don't need instructions. Eros is its own expression. In love, sex doesn't demand anything, because it has everything. In sex, love withholds nothing and receives everything.

Sexual energy is the energy of consciousness. When we are honest about it, we know nothing about sex, because we know nothing about consciousness. First, find awareness. Then let us find each other in that awareness, and let Eros dance.

sex and biology

Men and women need each other's
DNA. . . . Our sexual thought and
feelings are adapted to a world in
which sex led to babies, whether or not
we want to make babies now.

—STEVEN PINKER

THE SEXUAL DRIVE is the biological expression of the body's drive to reproduce. Is there more to it than that? Other than the biological drive, is there anything except ideas, realities created by clever minds?

We don't need to abstain from sex for enlightenment. There is no enlightenment; it is only a myth. But there is sex. It is undeniable. It wants to reproduce.

Biology is not concerned with our ideas. It is not concerned with our religion or our science. Biology is concerned only with our reproduction. The life that results is only a means to the end, the end being continued reproduction. What happens in between our birth and our participation in reproduction, our success or failure, our happiness or unhappiness, our fulfillment or lack, is just not a concern of biology.

Biology is not compassionate. It relentlessly drives the male and female to each other. It sweeps all obstructions out of its way. It doesn't care about birth control. Biology finds a way around all of that. It doesn't care about the individual person, and it doesn't care about the collective society. It cares only for its own. It cares only for the genetic material carried along, kept warm and alive, by the human hosts.

When we gaze longingly across the table at the inviting, candlelit face of our beloved, we may believe that we are the masters of our destiny and that the love we feel is the mystic love of the ages. But deep in the recesses of our being, the genetic matter is writing the script. The script urges us forward into the dance of reproduction that has as its sole purpose to never end. ❧

sex and religion

THE YOUNG MAN went to the monastery to learn about religion, God, and the fine craft of scribing. He spent many years working under an old monk, learning the art of hand copying and illuminating the old religious manuscripts.

One day it occurred to him to ask the old monk, "Father, how do we know that the text is accurate?"

The old monk answered, "We have used this text for many hundreds of years. Of course it is accurate."

A few days later the old monk came to the young apprentice and said, "You have provoked a serious question. I will spend the next days in isolation and study our sacred text."

After several days when the old monk did not appear, the young scribe went to his quarters where he found the old man bent over the text in tears.

"Father, what's wrong!" he cried.

Through his tears, the old scribe's voice was heard: "It was CEL-E-BRATE!"

the problem
with psychology

*Emotion, which is suffering, ceases to
be suffering as soon as we form a clear
and precise picture of it.*

—Spinoza

When we survey the wreckage that is often our relationships, the scarring of our interior world and the pain we cause others in our attempt to find contact, we will eventually seek help. In the Western culture this help has come to mean psychological counseling of one sort or another and, often, medication.

The problem with psychology is not that psychology doesn't work; it is that psychology addresses issues that, ultimately, are not at the core of our conflict.

We go to the psychological practitioner out of concern with our own integration and out of pain. We may find a Freudian, who will help us with our fixations; a Jungian, who will help us with our dreams; a Rogerian, who will listen to us. We may find a behaviorist, who will change our habits; a transpersonalist, who will expand our perspective; or a breath worker, who will take us through our blockages. We may find our way to a psychiatrist, who might alter our state of consciousness through medication; or a synthesist, who will offer a potpourri of techniques for our problems.

Regardless of where we go, we will be adjusted so that our conflict decreases. We will become better able to work, to play, to relate. We will become happy, our conflict gone. But, are we really happy? Is our conflict really gone?

It is like the mother who went to the psychiatrist to get help with her unmanageable son. The psychiatrist gave the woman some tranquilizers and instructed her to come back the following week with her son and he would work on the problem.

The next week the woman came into the office.

The psychiatrist asked her, "Has the boy gotten any better this week?"

"Who cares?"

We may become better adjusted to aspects of our life, but we still live in denial of the basic facts of our lives: we will die, but we have no inkling what death is; we do not live in love but rather in fear; we cannot still our lives long enough to examine anything; we haven't a glimmer of who we are. And, while we don't know who we are, we are sure that, at least, we *are*.

And that is the problem with psychology. It relates to the self as if it existed. This a priori concept of self sends us in the wrong direction.

Psychology defines the loss of self as a disorder. It approaches conflict as something to eradicate. This is all fine, if this model were true. But the model fails because nobody seems to know what the self is for, or, for that matter, where it is.

Psychology tries to find the self in the self's behavior. The psychologist tries to resolve conflict by resolving behavior. The approach may be to resolve conflict, to integrate memories, to understand compulsions, but ultimately all of this is to bring about a different behavior. This different behavior will allow greater acceptance and integration in the social organization of life.

We don't know what the self is, but we know how it should act in order to have a happy life. The self of psychology has relative existence. It manifests behavior, therefore it is.

The psychological practitioner works with this model of self. We go to the practitioner in conflict and never having considered the nature of our existential dilemma. The practitioner helps us see the psychological model, that is, the self as behavior. We understand that our behavior interacts with the social structures in our lives. If we can interact more fluidly, we will be more integrated.

We explore the constraints on our behavior, our childhood traumas, the influences of our parents, the unresolved problems of our life. We explore our body, our breath, our higher self. We do become more integrated. The self-behavior fits more fluidly with the social structure.

What is the problem with this? There is some relative value in social integration, after all.

For the psychologist to help us, we must first have a problem. Without the problem there can be no diagnosis, and without the diagnosis there can be no insurance billing. Without a problem there can be no legitimacy to the psychologist's work, no validation of the years of training and educational certification in problem solving. Without a problem the psychologist is at legal risk of malpractice.

The professional field of psychology cannot exist without our problems. The field of psychology revels in the discovery of new complexes, syndromes, and phobias. Its deepest desire is to be perceived as a rational, scientific field of thought. The massive machinery of psychological education and certification, research and clinical application depends on the public perception of empiricism. Psychologists love statistics and studies. Psychiatrists love mood-altering medicines and neurotransmitters. Nobody really wants to talk about the flaky edges of the field, the partially regulated underbelly of the field, the therapists. While many of these practitioners have the best of intentions, and a few of them are actually helpful, the rogue therapists can make it up as they go along. And, as long as they don't get sued out of business, they will stay in business. Even these quasi-scientific quacks adhere to psychology as pathology. That is the key entrance requirement to the club. If you want to treat or be treated, you have to have a problem.

Psychology has massive tomes filled with the symptoms that indicate each one of its diagnoses. Like a tabloid journalist with a deadline, the psychologist finds the story, whether there is one or not. The psychologist creates pathology where there once was life. The individual's story is replaced by the practitioner's story. But what is the story of psychology? Look into the bizarre world of Freud and his disciples/competitors. Would we want these people tinkering with our minds? Look into the brave new world of drug therapies, which has developed in the past fifty years. Do we really believe that we can find happiness in a pill? Have we ever met a psychology student who wasn't a lost soul looking for his or her own identity, looking for personal happiness? Have we ever met a psychologist who has found happiness?

So often the one who comes for help is overpowered by the diagnosis and succumbs to the pathogen injected into the patient's psyche by the so-called healer. Then the psychologist helps, by the hour, for a fee, to unravel the problem. But the problem is not actually our problem. This is the problem with psychology.

It is like the man who went to the doctor complaining that he hurt all over his body. Everywhere he touched himself he felt excruciating pain. His doctor was confounded and sent him to endless specialists. His symptoms, diagnosis, and prognosis were duly recorded by all according to their training. His problem, besides too many specialists, was of course, that he had a broken finger.

Our viewpoint is clouded. Everything it touches seems to hurt.

The problem is that our question is so much more profound than the response. The dilemma of our lives is far greater than the field of psychology can encompass. Yet psychology is willing to give us answers and even to provide us with drugs. Psychology is prepared to convince us that our resolution lies in joining this cult of confusion. And we join gladly. This cult, like all groups, gives us security, surety, and support. The price is small— ninety dollars an hour and our soul. Insurance will cover most of that.

If we step out of our sect, where will we go? How will we be supported? Will we go crazy, will we collapse, will we die?

We feel conflict. We cannot turn to psychology to explain it. We cannot fix it. We cannot make it go away. The conflict we feel is not a problem. It is a messenger.

The self is not the behavior. The behavior is conditioning. It is a personality we accepted early in our lives as a survival mechanism. It is absent of any intelligence and inherently empty, much like a computer program.

To resolve the conflict is impossible. Anything that makes us function better as an integrated self is a Band-Aid. By putting off the crisis, we create the pathology. We will function better, but the conflict will always be there. By suppressing the symptoms we drive them deeper into the psyche. Now we appear well adjusted, because our confusion is less accessible.

The conflict is existential. It is the friction between the bundle of ideas we call our self and the actuality of the boundarylessness of the world.

We cannot learn to integrate; we can only discover that we are integrated. The conflict is the guide. If it is covered over, we lose our way to this discovery.

No psychologist who takes away our conflict can help us with this discovery. No psychiatric drug, which buffers us from our conflict, can help us with this discovery. We do not need help; we need only understand that there is no choice in life but to follow the conflict where it takes us. If we are prepared to go there, we may discover the actuality of self and the end of our sorrow.

Are we prepared to look at the conflict in our marriage, in our workplace, in our home, in our family? Are we prepared to look at the conflict in our mind and body? Are we prepared to look at the conflict in our social structures, our churches and temples, our government, our schools?

If we are not, then we will call this conflict a problem and go to someone to help us resolve it. We will apply the temporary fix, again and again. We will get through our lives.

If we are prepared to look deeply at our conflict and not look away, we will discover that we are in a crisis of the spirit. Our life is on fire. Our life is falling away. Everything we have built and held dear is shattered. We have entered the dark night of the soul. We are prepared to die. And we are, for the first time in our lives, glimpsing freedom.

Those who would relieve us of our spiritual crisis—or pathologize it—are doing us a disservice. They, no doubt, shrank from their own dark night and found religion in psychology. Those who facilitate that crisis, while understanding that they can neither help us nor guide us, are the ones who have been there themselves.

The spiritual crisis, when it visits our lives, is the moment of profound change. It is the moment when we may come to the root of our pain, the source of our existential dilemma. We do not need to fix it, we do not need to run from it, we do not need to fear it. We do not need to do anything. In doing nothing we are left with an acute awareness of all that is occurring. An acute awareness of all that is occurring is, after all, what we are.

The macro-conditioning of an ego center, in relation to a world outside itself, changes in that awareness, as does the micro-conditioning of habit and personality. The fabric of our life changes. We discover that change, the very thing we were looking for, is the nature of this awareness. We discover that we are change itself. There is no self that is solid. There is no self that is located. There is only awareness and the expression of that awareness, which is change.

These notions are too extreme for psychology and for most of us. We are complacent in the dull ache of our lives. We use psychology to keep the ache numb when it flares into excruciating pain.

We don't demand of psychology that it resolve this pain for us once and for all. That would be asking too much. And psychology doesn't demand of us that we resolve this pain once and for all. That would be asking too much. We are in a codependent relationship with psychology. It is not a healthy relationship. Let us recognize that we need counseling.

Here is the one-minute counseling session. After this we are on our own. We don't have a problem, other than psychology. We don't need counseling. We are in conflict. Stay with that fact. That conflict is vibrating; it is shaking our world. Let our world shake. Let it tumble down. Whatever is left standing is life itself. Life is not in conflict.

Now, shall we live?

if I do absolutely nothing I would die

YOU CRITIQUE THERAPY and suggest doing nothing in response to conflict, and I must say that I don't know what you mean by this.

How do you find out what doing nothing means unless you do nothing?

But if I do absolutely nothing, I would die.

How do you know that?

Because that is what I have been told.

I am suggesting that you question what you have been told. Find out what is actually true.

And risk dying?

Risk everything.

I am still confused.

What is wrong with confusion?

What I am looking for in my life is a peaceful mind and an open heart. But instead, I am living over and over again my conditioned patterns, which I feel I cannot control. I would like to apply doing nothing to that, so that I am not just living out my life from beginning to end through conditioning.

What are you doing about that neurotic conditioning?

What is happening is that I am just becoming more and more frustrated as it keeps coming up. I don't feel I can control the frustration.

Then do nothing about that.

Then I just feel like I am boiling, angry, frustrated. I feel I need to express that, and so I end up getting angry at somebody or doing some activity to get rid of the stress of it all. I don't feel I can just sit with it.

Why not?

Because when I sit, then *that* becomes depression.

Who told you that?

I guess that is what I feel when I just sit. I can sit quietly when I am feeling good, but if I am feeling depressed, then I don't like that feeling.

So you are trying to get away from that feeling?

Yes.

That is really what you're doing—whatever is necessary to move away from this feeling of depression.

My goal is to feel good, happy, loving, warm, giving. That's the way I would like to be, but instead I find myself depressed, angry. That's not the totality, but with the life that I have lived, I should be perfectly happy. I have everything that I need. I have money, family, friends. I have good relationships, but still I experience sadness, jealousy, anger.

Which you're avoiding, not experiencing.

Which I do experience, but only for a short time, because I don't want to stay in that feeling.

And what would happen if you stayed in that feeling?

I guess I wouldn't die.

Maybe you would.

Maybe.

What I mean by doing nothing is that you do not avoid what is happening. It is being described in the negative because it is not an action. It is declining the action that avoids.

You're saying that whenever I am actively distracting myself, so that I don't have to feel those feelings, that I should sit down and meditate or be quiet? I still have to function in my life.

You are still looking for something to do.

My mind can't seem to grasp that. I feel I need a methodology.

What are the results the methodology is supposed to produce?

I want ways to not feel frustrated with the experience.

But you are frustrated. What you want is a methodology that lies to you, that says, "No, you are not frustrated." But you are.

I don't see any reason why I should be spending any part of my life being frustrated, when I have so much to give. I'd rather be out helping people.

You're positing something that is happening to you and through you, but that you don't want. It is as if you have been possessed by some other creature. What you are looking for now is a methodology by which you can expel this other creature, who is frustrated. There are a thousand methodologies out there by which you can divide yourself from yourself, create a positive and a negative "you," and try to put energy into the positive "you" and separate yourself from the negative "you." When you've done all that, don't you still have this positive and negative?

Should I just allow myself to experience these feelings and not get angry at myself that they are coming up, but just allow them to happen?

What choice do you have?

I suppose I don't have any choice.

The problem is not that you have frustration coming up or that you're experiencing what you say are negative qualities. That is not the problem at all. The problem is that you are identifying with the positive and the negative. You have this macro-conditioning that says you exist as an ego-center. You have this micro-conditioning that says you should be good. The macro and the micro are trying to sort out all the experiences that are arising so that they fit their description. Take that description away. Remove the conditioning for a moment and just look at what is actually happening. That is what I am suggesting that you do, by doing nothing. What is actually there? You won't find a good person or a bad person there. You won't find any person there. The frustration exists because you are trying to be something.

When anger comes up, I can express myself by either yelling or going for a run and doing something that physically expresses that anger. Or I can just say, "OK, it's not me, it's not anything, just let it go." But, if I just let it go, am I not suppressing my anger? I am often confused as to whether to express it or to repress it.

You have divided yourself into multiple components now. You have the anger, you have the question of whether to suppress or to express, and you have the confusion that arises. What if you do nothing? Anger arises and you don't do anything. Then what happens?

I am afraid that I will repress the anger, that it will stay in my stomach, and that then I will get cancer and die. When I have watched other family members repress their anger and their feelings, the result has been death by cancer. That has become my fear.

This is your thought process. This is doing something. This is the idea that you need to find out what to do. This is your addiction. You find out that you're living your life in fear. And that is doing something. You are saying, "OK, I don't want to die of cancer, therefore I am going to do something about this anger. What shall I do? Shall I express it? Shall I release it? I am confused. I don't know." This is all thought process. What is actually happening? You don't know, because it has been lost. What actually happens when anger arises and you do absolutely nothing in relationship to that anger?

What happens for me is that it builds in me, more and more, until I explode.

That is because you are doing something. You are feeding that anger with the energy of your own thoughts, obsessing about it. Now, we have anger and we have uncontrolled thoughts about anger. What if you don't do anything about that? What happens? This is where you have to go into this yourself. You have to find out by your own direct view. I can use words here, but I don't think that is going to be helpful.

How would I know when I am doing nothing?

You won't know. The knower won't know because the knower won't be there. Doing nothing is a natural state where there is no doer. There is nobody to deal with anger. There is no one to suppress it or express it. There is no one to explode.

There is no one to get cancer. And there is really no anger. Anger is a word. And attached to that word is a whole string of your conditioning. The actuality is the movement of energy that does not have a center. You are trying to approach something that you have created, and that has been created through your own education and conditioning. You are trying to approach it through additional creations of your mind. That is the doer.

Anger is where thought blocks energy. It is constriction on the movement of energy. Thought, which is a constriction on energy, asks how to further constrict energy so that constriction won't take place. You can't approach it from your mind, because your mind is the problem. You will go around in circles endlessly until you recognize that. You cannot constrict energy and find expansion. You can just do nothing. It is energy. It is innately expressing.

How can I have a relationship with another person like that?

How can you have a relationship that is not like that?

But what are the agreements, the conditions, the expressions that two people will live by?

The agreement is that we don't know what relationship is. The conditions are that we are discovering what actuality is in each moment. The expression is the beauty that occurs when two people stop managing the relationship and get out of the way of love.

What keeps a relationship together with such an approach?

Nothing keeps it together. This relationship exists in freedom and without containment. There is no risk of loss, because we do not own or control it in the first place. There is no place else for love to go but where it is. Where it is, is everywhere.

Then what is it that brings two people together?

Isn't the question, What is it that appears to take two apart? Isn't the illusion of separation the mystery? The fact of being one is our natural state. We are born from it and die in it. Why do we live as if we are separate?

How do I realize this?

Realization requires believing in separation, believing in some process or knowledge that will end that division and move you through time and effort to achieve the resolution that you imagine awaits you. Effort and time only push realization farther away, so a life of realization will be a very busy life, a life of continuous becoming. Being one requires nothing. It is immediately present. We have already arrived, because we have never left.❧

community
and family

Three things in human life are important. The first is to be kind. The second is to be kind. And the third is to be kind.

—HENRY JAMES

WE DON'T BEAR children out of love. Let us be honest about this one thing, if nothing else.

We bear children out of confusion, out of desire, out of our ideas, out of our need for security. Mostly, we don't really consider why we bear children; we just do it. Our biology is driving us. The genetic material is demanding continuity and embodiment.

But we don't bear children out of love. We could not express love in this way—in giving birth to a child who will live in the pain of the world that we have never resolved. Love would not make this child the beneficiary of our confusion and fear.

We call the deep feeling for our children love, but it is attachment. Love is something else altogether.

We may find that this attachment is the gateway to love, but more likely we will find the attachment to our children the gateway to hell. Attachment may function to protect the child as it grows. That is fine. Protect the child. But the same attachment will scar the child and us when we cannot let go.

Love does not produce children, but love must raise them. And, in the end, love will let them go. We cannot raise our children. If we do, they will be like us. What a tragedy that would be. Instead, let us get out of the way entirely. Let love raise our children.

Out of our confusion we have created the child. Now we must really take ourselves out of our confusion to raise the child. If there were spiritual work, this would be it. The demand is total and unrelenting. The sacrifice is the entirety of our conditioning. The penalty for failure is another conditioned generation in the endless chain of human misery.

In infancy we are the slaves of the child. The newborn depends entirely on us to provide its needs. Its cry is a question. Answering it, we create the basis for the child's security and the possibility of the child's own discovery. This preverbal stage is the period when much of the personality unfolds.

We will need to provide an environment of freedom and spaciousness as the child develops its language, identity, and will. In this environment the child is a demand for full contact, intimate relationship, the very thing we say we want but seem actually to fear.

We will be tempted to try to make the child fit into our world, into our schedule, into our patterns. We will be tempted to condition the child, to socialize the child, to create the rules that have been fed into our own minds.

The child learns from our being, not from our words. The child observes the qualities that are actively manifest in our lives. If there is a "do," let us do that. If there is a "don't," let us not do that. Let us live our advice to our children. Let us demonstrate the possibilities of a loving existence.

The child will be directed by its inner volition, its inherent interests and qualities. The embedded biological memory of genetic material will interact with the environmental forces, and the child's nature will spontaneously emerge.

Later, the child can be liberated from the notion that we are the parents. Free from this idea, the child steps forward into the life of an adult. The relationship with the parent now only exists if there is mutuality, not out of obligation or guilt.

How this sort of child, now an adult, raises the next generation may be fundamentally different. How this adult interacts with the world around may be fundamentally different. We do not know, because we are not that. We know nothing about what a free human being would do or be.

We cannot produce transformed children by our intent. We can, however, leave our mental "gunk" out of the child-rearing business. We can absent our conditioned center from the process.

We have seen what happens when parents inject their conditioning into their children, because we are those children. Now, let us see what children will be like if we leave ourselves, our past, our conditioning out of child raising altogether.

For those who insist on having children, there are plenty already here. They are all over the world, abandoned, uncared for, destitute. Let us go get these children. Let us raise them. Then we will have children. We won't be creating more; we'll be taking care of what's here already.

Why is that not good enough for us? Why must we reproduce, create yet more children? Is our biological imperative so much greater than our need to understand it? The self reproduces; it hopes for continuity and security in its biological offspring. The self wants the experience of birth, of motherhood, of fatherhood.

Meanwhile, children play in garbage heaps and die of disease, starvation, and hopelessness. Those who survive will have their own children of destitution.

And our children will look the other way and have their own children. Children of privilege. Children who have learned to look the other way.

We will produce children. This is our nature. This is not bad. There does not need to be guilt or confusion around this. Children are wonderful, beautiful creatures. Produce children, adopt children, mentor children, but let us not inject our conditioning into them. Let them be what they are—free.

While we are at it, let us leave our family structure out of child raising as well. After all, we don't really know what a family is. Is family defined by biology, by convention, by religion?

Historically, family has been defined by the marriage of man and woman, the combining of their assets, and the preservation of their children. These norms were enforced by the religious tradition, by cultural mores, and by law. Now this form of family is undergoing radical redesign. In the developed world marriage is followed by divorce and remarriage. Assets are partitioned, distributed by prenuptial agreements, or divided by the decree of a divorce court.

The hold of religion over these matters is slipping. Social traditions are changing. Law is being constantly re-created. In the United States the phrase *normal family* has become an oxymoron. The abnormal has become the norm. Those who have never divorced and who are married with their own biological children are the aberration.

Is family, in its true sense, the grouping of multigenerational people out of love?

Perhaps traditional families don't work. If families produced happy beings, we wouldn't be in this mess. We've had thousands of years of families.

The right of parents to control their children is in constant struggle throughout the world with the rights of the state. Neither right is authentic. The state has no rights over the child, nor should the parent have that control. The rights belong to the child. We are the protectors, the custodians of these rights—the rights of the child to nutrition, housing, clothing, education, love, and freedom.

Strip away, for a moment, the religious and social overlay that reinforces families and describes their virtues.

What is underneath? Two adults, bored and angry with each other; children isolated and sad; grandparents abandoned to loneliness and uselessness. Free them all from the constraints that bind them—the parents, the grandparents, the children. Now let the form change.

Unhappy adults move away from each other, looking for love. Unhappy children look for guidance and security. Unhappy grandparents look for contact and function. What if the basic social unit is based instead on these qualities: love, security, guidance, contact, and function? The family unit ceases to be defined by a monogamous couple and their biological children, with Grandma in the attic or the nursing home.

Now we can consider a multi-generational configuration that bases its existence on its own actual and perceived mutuality. Perhaps this configuration lives in a house or a cluster of houses. It may be a single person, a traditional family, an extended family, a polygamous or polyandrous family, a commune, or a village. Its structure emerges out of interior feeling rather than the pressures of society, family, or religion. Its qualities are unknown because the actual potential of human relatedness is unknown. We really only know that the present structures have failed. They cannot be saved, nor should they be saved. They are based on the past, and now we are all somewhere else.

And why do we marry? Do we fear relationship so much that we must constrain it by legal ties?

Marriage is the function of pressure—societal, family, religious. Its purpose is to stabilize our social structures. Marriage has nothing to do with love and relationship.

We cannot own another. We cannot control another. The pressures of law and society do not make a marriage. Marriage is the direct experience of the boundaryless nature of life. Then, with or without the acknowledgment of society, there is marriage.

That relationship is all of our relationship to each other. We are all married. Only a few recognize that, only a few express that relatedness in the intimacy of living together, coordinating the life functions and material sustenance.

Marriage cannot thrive without the universal aspect. A marriage that is two against the world is devoured by its own limited perspective, self-centeredness, and fear. Yet this is what we are told to aspire to. This is the form that is promulgated by film and literature. It is romanticized. It is canonized.

This exclusive marriage must protect itself from intrusion at all costs. No man or woman outside the marriage can dare to experience the intimacy within this exclusive marriage for fear of shattering it. No child other than the biological progeny can be included. No elder can be involved except, perhaps, reluctantly, the biological grandparents.

The exclusive marriage exists to protect itself, to provide for the surviving spouse and the children of that marriage. It recognizes and interacts with the world around it only so far as that world enhances the exclusivity of the marriage. The exclusive marriage exists in denial of its own failures, its own inherent unhappiness, its own lack of creativity and utility.

The exclusive marriage ultimately fails more than it succeeds, but it continues. It continues because we are asleep and cannot conceive of any other way. The exclusive marriage is a marriage of fear.

But there is another way. It is the freedom that arises out of aloneness. Awake, we cannot forge exclusivity in our relationships; we can only relate in freedom and responsibility. Exclusive marriage transforms into inclusive marriage. This is marriage that is open and intimate with all that it encounters. Some who encounter each other will stay, living together, sharing resources and responsibilities. Some will relate, but from their own circumstances. The possible forms are many, the essence is only one—open and inclusive.

This inclusiveness can occur as the expression of the life of one, the life of a couple, the life of multiple individuals.

These inclusive marriages—naturally occurring, multi-generational, intimate groupings—do not exist in isolation. By their nature these marriages relate to each other as tribes, or villages, or ultimately as urban clusters.

From the sum of these groupings can emerge a new culture, the culture of inclusion.

❧

The forms that our lives take—our family, our schools, our churches, our society—are all unconscious, preconceived hand-me-downs. This is our reality; this is the realm in which we struggle, in which we are failures or successes.

The rat in the psychologist's maze succeeds when it gets to the other side, pushes the lever, and gets rewarded with a food pellet. This is our life. The maze is the labyrinth of thought—the collective, societal thought. Is this enough for us?

To step outside this maze is not a small thing. Every form exerts its force upon us. The pressure is immense. If we take even the smallest step, our world begins to unwind.

This is not something to take lightly. Let us look around our life. Are we prepared for all that we are, all that we identify with, to fall away and for something entirely new to emerge? That is the price we will pay. There is no negotiation. Nor is there any turning back.❧

belief
and uncertainty

*It is true, that which I have revealed
to you; there is no God, no universe,
no human race, no earthly life, no
heaven, no hell. It is all a dream—a
grotesque and foolish dream. Nothing
exists but you. And you are but a
thought—a vagrant thought, a
useless thought, a homeless thought,
wandering forlorn among the empty
eternities!*

—MARK TWAIN

WE ARE ALREADY immersed in spirituality by the simple act of living.

Is it possible that there is no separate spiritual life to live? Could it be that the life of spirit is the invention of romantic self-indulgence? After all, life doesn't require an overlay of our ideas. Life is everything, totality. It doesn't get more spiritual than totality.

114

This is a disquieting consideration for those of us on our chosen spiritual path, those who have invested so much time and energy in applying our beliefs to our lives. It is a particularly disturbing consideration for those whose profession, livelihood, and identification are teaching others how to live the spiritual life.

If we are already bathing in spirit, then we don't actually need a religion, church, or ritual.

Yet, our world is full of religious institutions. Some of these attempt to embody the mysticism that emanates from life. Perhaps these vibrant religious structures reflect the intensity of those who animate them. But more often, forms of religious expression are mired in blind habit and the pursuit of power.

We can only be lured into the world of stagnant spirituality if we are convinced that we are in a divided world. If we are in a world of good and bad, sinner and saint, reward and punishment, then we are compelled to seek the institution, the teacher, the philosophy which will guarantee that we come down on the right side in life, and more important, in death. We seek to end our personal uncertainty by blindly accepting the absolute knowledge of belief.

But uncertainty and belief are a divided world only in thought. In actuality they are the same. Belief cannot exist without uncertainty. Good cannot exist without bad. The saints of the world would be unemployed without sin. All of these dualistic qualities are codependent. If we see the codependence, the dualism ceases. These are not two distinct qualities, but rather aspects of the same.

How do we formulate our church, then? We can no longer divide ourselves into believer and God, into parish and priest, into members and outsiders. Everything our mind tries to cling to slips from our grasping. We cannot find the beginning of our church and its end; we cannot find that which is spiritual and that which is not.

If life is whole, nothing is spiritual. And everything is spiritual. Our conditioning is spiritual, our anger is spiritual, our stupidity is spiritual. Why is there no spiritual teacher who is showing us techniques for cultivating our conditioning, our anger, our stupidity? Why are we always instructed on how to move from our failed life to the life of glory?

What if none of it is true? What if our failed life and the life of glory are both fictions of the religious mind? What if we are left with just the bare fact of our life, the raw spirit of what is occurring, without interpretation and without an interpreter?

In a teaching tale the Rabbi is asked the difference between the righteous and the wicked person.

"The truth is," replied the Rabbi, "that both the righteous and the wicked constantly commit sins, but as long as the righteous lives he knows he is sinning and as long as the wicked sins he knows he is living."

But the mystic would reply that there is a life that is neither righteous nor wicked.

Mystics of every religious tradition have discovered this life without opposites at the frontier of their own spiritual structures. This collapse of the known, the end of effort, the dark night of the soul, where even the most heartfelt prayer goes unanswered, is the end of the world of duality. This collapse is the end of religion, because it is the end of the self. It is the end of hope, the end of the spiritual quest, the end of meaning. It is absolute darkness, a world without distinction.

But even this collapse is not the end, because it, too, collapses. This collapse of the collapse becomes an explosion of love, the expression of God in the supplicant, the formless in the form. There is no God to which to call, because God is already expressing fully through the mystic. There is no one to call to God, because the mystic cannot find the one who was once separate.

Now, the religious forms and rituals are infused with the actuality of boundless love, and the mystic returns to the life of prayer and devotion. Now, the religious form is the expression of totality.

If we will have a church, a temple, a place of religious expression, can we make it about this? Can we build a church of mysticism? We can practice our spirituality not just in special places on special days, but rather in the ordinariness of our day-to-day activity.

What if we remove the dogma, the myth, the clergy, the promises, and the security? Do we really need arbitration between ourselves and life? Can we stand alone in the midst of life and look directly at its nature, at our nature? Can we live a life that is innately good without the reward of future salvation to motivate us?

If we can, then let us.

If we cannot, then let us be honest about our own fear and selfishness. If we cannot, then let us understand that our real religion is the worship of ourselves, our survival, our pleasure, our security. Leave God out of it.❧

thought, reality, and the Internet

How DOES CONNECTED thought occur between two people?

Thought is reality. We share reality. We share thought.

How is it being initiated? Where is it coming from? All of a sudden a thought pops into my mind—I need to call a particular person—and then suddenly the phone rings and it is that person.

Your thought, the person's thought, and the phone ringing is all the same thought.

But there is another person who is not phoning, and I am also thinking about that person.

That is a self-explanatory event. If there is no phone call, there is no thought. If there is no thought, there is no reality.

I must also be blocking out thoughts. Why is it that every time the phone rings, I am not thinking about that person?

Because it does not fit into your reality. Your reality is a very constricted reality. You have been trained to think rationally. You have been trained to think that you are an individual who is separate from what is around you. That is your reality. Your reality does not allow for, nor does it express, interconnectedness.

I can do that.

You can do that, but you'll lose your center. What if the world is, in fact, constructed so that thought is reality? When you think "friend," the phone rings. What will you do with that? In that world, when you think "war," somebody pushes a button and sends a bomb. When you think "anger," then somebody has a heart attack. When you think "greed," somebody goes bankrupt and the money shows up in your hands. Can you handle that?

No, because I can't control my thoughts, and my thoughts are not all pure love.

Think of it as the Internet. You have your log-on code, and you have your e-mail address. That is you. From that you can access other people. Your message can be on their computer at the same time it is on your computer. You can both be reading the same message at the same time. That message essentially exists in the entire Internet simultaneously. Others, from any cyber-location, could go into that area and find that message, but they are not in that area. They are in their own areas, talking to the people they want to talk to.

In that Internet doesn't all information, all Internet reality, exist all the time? Can't you access anything that you want in that Internet all the time? Of course, the problem with accessing everything all the time is that it would be too much. You would run out of storage space. You would not be able to read it all.

That is when we start to become overwhelmed by life. When we get off the plane in a third-world country and start experiencing the starvation, the pain, the poverty, the sadness. We are feeling everything, and then we realize that we can't feel it because it is too much to handle. We shut down and then we concentrate on the next thing we need to do for ourselves.

That is the way we construct reality.

Is there also a way to access a particular person? Can I actually sit down and send out a telepathic message to a person?

Why not?

I feel that I can do that with some, but other people are distracted.

If they are not "checking their e-mail," then they are not going to get the message. And the further problem is that in the Internet people can create entire worlds. There are complex virtual environments with created characters all interacting with one another, with their created personalities, desires, problems, and so forth. And people can get very wrapped up in that world.

The problem comes when you forget that you are in the Internet. You forget that you are in a computer network, a web of machine-generated reality. You forget that your e-mail address is just an address, or that the world in which you are interacting is a created world.

The difficulty comes when you lose awareness. The same with reality. You have forgotten that you are in the web of thought. You have forgotten that your name, your form, the idea you identify with so vigorously, are really just your address at this moment. We have collectively created this reality, but we have forgotten that it is just a virtual reality. We have forgotten that we have identified with being American or some other nationality; man or woman; Catholic, Protestant, Jewish, or Muslim. And so we have conflicts, wars with others who believe just as firmly in their identifications.

The further question is what happens when you remember that it is just the Internet, just a created virtual reality, just a computer and an e-mail address? What happens when you remember that your life, your ideas, your very identity are a creation of thought? And what happens when, after hours or days or years inside this virtual reality, you reach over and switch off the computer? What happens when your mind falls quiet for a moment? What do you discover? This is the challenge.

what is relationship?

WHAT DO YOU mean by relationship—relationship to what or between whom? What is relationship?

Relationship is the state. It is a noun. Look it up in the dictionary. It will define relationship as "the state of being related." It doesn't say to what. Relationship is not in motion, it is not looking, it is not craving. It exists in absolute stillness without any source and without any object. Relationship is not to anyone or anything; it is not between any two. The mysterious alchemy of that stillness is this—by not being related "to" or "between," relationship becomes the expression of everything. Relationship is not to totality, it is totality. This is why so many mystics have discovered that the limitation of worship is that they must maintain the separation from that which they love.

Then what do you mean by the addiction of separation?

The mystic is tempted by his love for God, even after he discovers that maintaining that duality separates him from the totality, which, of course, is the manifest God. So the poor mystic is in a real dilemma. He's been fasting and praying and doing all kinds of austerities for all these years. He loves his God with all his heart. He prays to God every hour of every day. God returns his worship with words of love. One day he asks God for insight into the nature of the absolute and the boundaryless nature of life is revealed to him. God shows the mystic that the God he worships is the mind's projection. God shows the mystic that there is no mystic who worships, and no God to be worshiped. There is no separation. There is no difference. The mystic is in rapture. He calls to God his thanks, his praise, his everlasting love. But, there is only silence in response.

In the mystic's realization of nonduality God has vanished.

So, after a very long night of consideration of the unity of life, the mystic calls to God once more. This time he asks for one last boon. The mystic asks God to take away the knowledge of that true nature of life and to return as his object of love.

Of course the boon is granted. The mystic once again can worship his God. He soon forgets the totality.

In our lives we have built our social constructions around our separation. These are the concepts through which we organize and communicate our reality. We have forgotten the totality of our existence, and yet the pain of our lives, the gnawing emptiness, and the compulsion to fill that emptiness, are reminders that there is something beyond separation. But we can never remain still enough to see what is beyond. We can never quiet our minds or our lives. We are addicted to separation.

You talk about the fear of the unknown being the projection of the memory of our failures, our hurts, our anxieties. Don't we learn from our past experiences? Isn't there a difference between irrational fear and knowing that when I touch a hot pan I am going to get burned?

We are not talking about knowing not to touch a hot pan. This is information, not fear. We are not even talking about the caution of touching a pan because it may be hot. This is intelligence.

We are talking about what the mind does with this information as it searches endlessly, relentlessly, for the action that will have no possibility of touching a hot pan. We are talking about the mind that projects the possibility of a hot pan everywhere.

The mind has developed as an instrument of survival. It calculates the likelihood of survival in each action. This worked well thousands of years ago on the savannah. There we had to get to the tree with the fruit before the lion got to us. Our minds calculated. The good minds made it. The not-so-good minds got gobbled up by the lions. The good minds reproduced and got better.

Now this mind has developed into a monster. It cannot stop calculating whether or not the lions are going to eat us. Of course, there are no lions. There are automobiles going through intersections, checkbooks to balance, phones to answer, planes crashing, MTV, fast food—in short, an accelerated world where we don't know friend from foe. We can't tell where the lions are. We can't tell where the pans are, let alone which are hot. Our minds are trying to calculate our survival under the crushing weight of information overload.

Faced with this overload the mind projects danger everywhere. It becomes neurotic. It lives in fear. It no longer knows what it fears. It doesn't make any difference. Fear ensures survival, and survival is the mind's game.

You say that our biggest fear is the fear of death. Is that true for very religious people who see death as the passage to eternal life and happiness or whatever their beliefs may describe?

For those, the fear is the loss of their belief system. The identification with their beliefs has become so strong that the loss of the belief system is their death. Fear of death is not just the fear of the death of the body but rather loss of the identification with a center.

For most of us that identification is primarily with our body, and so death of the body is the threat. But for some there is primary identification with ideology. And for many the religious belief is an unexamined conditioning or a backup plan to a life lived entirely materialistically.

ten things we can do to begin relating

 1. DON'T PAY ATTENTION to lists that tell you what to do with your life or tell you that you can change yourself in ten steps. That includes this list.

2. Start being honest and don't stop. Start with yourself. Include everyone in your life.

3. Begin your day by reflecting on your own death. This is the last day of your life. Are you living?

4. Begin your day by reflecting on your own birth. This is the first day of your life. Are you creating, growing?

5. Begin your day by reflecting on the fact that your essence was never born and so cannot die. There is no day. There is just this moment. This has always been true. This will always be true.

6. Don't think for five minutes. Discover what happens.

7. Don't move for ten minutes. Discover what happens.

8. Breathe—simply breathe—for twenty minutes. Discover what happens.

9. Eat when you are hungry, and no more than what satisfies that hunger. Drink when you are thirsty, and no more than what quenches that thirst. Sleep when you are tired, and only until you are rested.

10. Pay attention to the deep resistance of the mind to living these simple things. See Number 1 in this list. Discard this list. ❧

beyond relationship,
beyond love

*When on one side we place all the
actions of this life and on the other
silence, we find that it weighs down
the scales.*

ST. ISAAC THE SYRIAN

THERE IS no such thing as relationship, because
there is no one to relate from and there is no one to
relate to. There is no such thing as love because there is
no one to act out of love and no one to be the object of
that love.

How can this be? We certainly feel that we are in
relationship, that we are in love. There is the other, someone we can see and touch. There is someone we can
amuse, we can flirt with, we can argue and fight with.

Of course we are in relationship. Certainly we are
in love.

But, wait a moment.

Take away the thought, the idea of the other. Take away the image. Now look without these ideas, in silence, at the other.

Is the other inside or outside your gaze? Is the world inside or outside your perception? Does anything divide the world into inside and outside, into two?

Thought arises, and with it the world is split into two. This world of the "me" and the other exists in thought and is created by thought, by language, by conditioning.

Thought cannot love. Thought can only think. Thought can think of love, it can speak of love, it can imagine love, but it cannot love.

That which divides the universe cannot perceive itself and so cannot see the undivided world.

Love arises when thought does not. We cannot stop thought, nor can we create love. This is simply because we ourselves are thought forms.

Thought cannot bring its own end, and love will not compete.

This is the paradox in which we reside, waiting for our own cessation. This is not the cessation of our physicality, or of thought, but the cessation of the identification with that physicality and with that thought. It is the cessation of the idea of continuity, of solidity, of location.

There is absolutely nothing we can do to bring about the love. We are seduced by our separation. We exist only in our distinction. We don't know how to create anything but our isolation.

In separation we can relate, we can objectify, we can become attached, adoring, infatuated with the object of our affection.

We cannot love.

And we cannot do anything to change that. Nor can anyone do anything to change us.

Give up all hope of love.

Give up all projections of love.

Give up.

Love is the fire that burns us. We cannot survive; we cannot be there when something new emerges from the ashes, takes wing, and flies. This is why although we say we want love, in fact, we fear love.

Give up.

Give up not because life is hopeless, but because hope projects, through thought, into the fire and obscures the actuality.

Life is not hopeless. We are hopeless. We cannot escape into the realm of ideas, although we will try. And we cannot move forward without hope.

We are caught.

We are still.

a challenge to relate

*I beg your pardon. I didn't recognize
you. I've changed a lot.*

—OSCAR WILDE

WHAT WOULD OUR life be like, what would our world be like, if we gave expression to the fullness of relationship? What if we valued the connection with the world around us as much as we now value our separation?

No matter how much money and security, fame and glory we stockpile in our lives, we live in pain when we live in separation. In just one moment of reflection this is clear. Yet we live our lives to ensure that we never have that one moment of reflection. We run hard from what we already know.

The challenge we face is not a difficult one. It does not require more from us than what we have. It simply requires everything.

There are many reasons we may give for refusing this challenge. The mind, conditioned as it is to its own survival, will always find a rationale for separation.

Indeed, there is only one reason for us to take up the challenge of relationship, but it is a compelling one—we must fully relate if we are to fully live.

There is ample evidence of the failure and destruction brought about by the theology of separation, the worship of self. Now, is it possible to give expression to the possibilities inherent in our relatedness? Can we dedicate our lives to the whole?

Each of us must face our own reactions, our fear, our own addiction to separation. In standing absolutely still in the midst of our conflicted, conceptual world, we may discover the explosion of unity, of love, that is the bare actuality of life.

Here is the challenge. Stop. Look. Listen.

Nothing is in the way.

Spontaneously, life is bursting forth.

Those interested may write:

Steven Harrison
P.O. Box 6071
Boulder, CO 80306
Email: InDialog@aol.com
Web site: http://www.doingnothing.com

❧

All author profits from this book will be donated to
nonprofit organizations, including:

All Together Now International
P.O. Box 7111
Boulder, CO 80306
Email: AllToNow@aol.com
Website: http://www.alltogether.org

A.T.N.I. supports projects designed not only to address
material needs but to foster self-sufficiency, cooperation,
and community. Current programs are focused in Tibet,
Nepal, and India.